Avisson Young Adult Series

Daredevils of the Air
Thrilling Tales of Pioneer Aviators

Karen E. Bledsoe

Avisson Press Inc.
Greensboro

Copyright © 2003 by Karen E. Bledsoe. All rights reserved. For information, contact Avisson Press Inc., P.O. Box 38816, Greensboro, NC 27438 USA.

First Edition   Printed in the USA

Library of Congress Cataloging- in- Publication Data

Bledsoe, Karen E.
  Daredevils of the air : thrilling tales of pioneer aviators / Karen E. Bledsoe.
       p. cm. -- (Avisson young adult series)
  Summary: Reviews the exploits of a number of early aviators, including the Wright Brothers, Glenn Curtiss, Harriet Quimby, Eddie Rickenbacker, Bessie Coleman, and Amelia Earhart.
  Includes bibliographical references and index.
     ISBN 1-888105-58-5 (pbk.)
  1. Air pilots--Biography--Juvenile literature. 2. Aeronautics--History--Juvenile literature. 3. Aeronautics--Records--Juvenile literature. [1. Air pilots. 2. Aeronautics--History. 3. Flight.] I. Title. II. Series.
  TL539.B54 2003
  629.13'092'2--dc22

                                            2003052055

Photo Credits: Pages 100, 103, 120, 137, 140, courtesy of AP / Wide World Photos. Page 24, courtesy Curtiss Museum, Hammondsport, New York. Pages 9, 13, 35, 52, Library of Congress. Cover: Library of Congress, Prints and Photographs Division; LC-DIG-ppprs-00701, LC-DIG-ppprs-00692, LC-USZ62-127779.

Efforts have been made to ascertain the copyright holders, if any, of images in this book. Anyone who believes they have not been properly credited should contact the publisher, above, so that proper credit can be given.

Contents

Introduction 5

Chapter 1: Quiet Triumph at Kitty Hawk —
The Wright Brothers 7
Chapter 2: A Brazilian in Paris —
Alberto Santos-Dumont 17
Chapter 3: From June Bugs to Flying Boats —
Glenn Curtiss 22
Chapter 4: The Master Birdman — Lincoln Beachey 33
Chapter 5: The Race Across the English Channel—
Louis Blériot and Hubert Latham 45
Chapter 6: Across America, Crash by Crash —
Cal Rodgers 50
Chapter 7: A Woman's Place is in the Cockpit —
Harriet Quimby 61
Chapter 8: Wild Warbirds — Eddie Rickenbacker 71
Chapter 9: Queen of the Barnstormers —
Bessie Coleman 78
Chapter 10: Flying *Old Soggy* — "Slats" Rodgers 88
Chapter 11: From Airmail to the Atlantic —
Charles Lindbergh 99
Chapter 12: For the Fun of It — Amelia Earhart 109

Chapter 13: Wings Across Africa — Beryl Markham **125**
Chapter 14: Mid-Air Oil Change — Charles Kingsford-Smith and P.G. Taylor **134**
Chapter 15: "Wrong Way" Gets His Wish — Douglas Corrigan **141**

Where to Learn More **152**
Index **154**

Thrilling Tales of Early Aviators

Introduction

One hot August morning, the air over Chicago was filled with the roar of strange new machines — flying machines. The international airshow brought American, English, and French pilots to Chicago where they demonstrated their skill and daring in speedy little hand-built airplanes. Spectators thrilled to watch the aviators set records for speed, distance, altitude, and stunts. Lincoln Beachey flew to a record 11,578 feet in a Curtiss biplane, spiraled gracefully down, and climbed stiffly out, limbs numb from the freezing cold. Cal Rodgers, in a Wright biplane, set a duration record of three hours and thirty minutes. These records may not sound like much until you consider that the year was 1911, just eight years after the Wright Brothers flew the first working airplane. The crafts flown in the Chicago airshow were rickety structures of wood and canvas, hardly more than box kites with engines and propellers.

Beachey, Rodgers, Curtiss, and the Wright Brothers are among the pioneers of aviation you will read about in this book. Their stories, and tales of other daring pilots, tell of the excitement and danger of early aviation. Some pilots were purely entertainers, some worked hard to make aviation practical for everyone. Some deliberately sought danger, while some found themselves in peril despite their careful preparation. Triumph and tragedy, determination and daring are all part of the saga of early aviation.

Ready for adventure? Put on your helmet and goggles,

your leather jacket and white silk scarf. Fly away with the men and women who first opened the skies for all, whose amazing stories hardly seem possible to those of us with our feet still firmly on the ground.

Chapter 1
Quiet Triumph at Kitty Hawk
— The Wright Brothers

The Airship That Really Flies" read the headline of the tiny article on the front page of the *South Bend Tribune* on December 18, 1903, one of the few newspapers that actually printed the incredible announcement. The residents of South Bend, Indiana, barely reacted the announcement which would, within ten years, change the face of the globe forever:

> Norfolk, Va, Dec. 18 — A successful trial of a flying machine was made yesterday near Kitty Hawk, N.C., by Wilbur and Orville Wright, of Dayton, O[hio]... The machine has no balloon attachment but gets its force from propellers worked by a small engine.

Earlier in the same year, Samuel P. Langley, the eminent scientist and secretary of the Smithsonian Institution, had attempted to fly a propeller-driven winged craft. Newspaper reporters came flocking when they heard the announcement. Langley's *Aerodrome*, its engines sputtering and propellers spinning, was catapulted down a track not to a triumphant flight, but to an ignoble plunge into the Potomac River. Two more times Langley tried to fly his machine, and two more times he failed.

"The flying machine which will really fly," declared *The New York Times*, "might be evolved by the combined and continuous efforts of mathematicians and mechanicians in from one to ten million years." The newspapers stated, and nearly everyone agreed, that humans simply weren't meant to fly.

Small wonder, then, that the world ignored the tiny announcement in the *South Bend Tribune* and the few other papers that bothered to print it. How could anyone believe that two unknown brothers from Ohio could succeed where the great and learned Samuel P. Langley had failed?

But humans had been flying for over one hundred years. Hot-air balloons were invented in France by the Montgolfier brothers in 1783, and were followed quickly by the invention of gas balloons in the same year. Balloons were being used as spy devices in war and for scientific exploration in the upper atmosphere. The problem with balloons, though, was that they were at the mercy of the winds. Even propeller-driven dirigibles wallowed out of control in strong breezes. Inventors dreamed of creating a flying craft that flew under its own power and could be steered wherever the pilot wanted to go.

The trail to the first airplane was blazed by Otto Lilienthal, a German inventor. Lilienthal was an engineer whose firm manufactured small steam engines and marine signal devices. He was fascinated by bird flight and made extensive studies of how birds flew, eventually publishing a paper on the subject. Lilienthal was convinced that if an artificial wing could be perfected, people could fly as freely as birds. Lilienthal experimented with wings of wood and fabric, and designed the world's first glider. He

Orville (left) and Wilbur Wright, the famous brothers who first achieved heavier than air flight, in 1903.

designed, built, and tested eighteen different gliders in all. Most of them were beautiful, eliptical-winged structures which were flown like today's hang-gliders. In 1896,

Lilienthal was killed when one of his gliders crashed on a test flight.

Langley had studied Lilienthal's designs when he constructed his Aerodrome. His design was based on sound research. Later experiments by airman Glenn Curtiss would prove that the Aerodrome would have flown if Langley hadn't used a catapult to launch it. Had Langley let his machine launch by its own power, the course of history would have been changed.

For while Lilienthal experimented with gliders and Langley struggled to make the world's first airplane, unknown to either of them two young brothers in the United States were avidly following their progress. Orville and Wilbur Wright, though barely out of their teens, were already veteran inventors. As boys they had invented a rudder-guided sled, an improved kite, and a machine for folding letters and handbills. As teenagers they had assembled a small printing press for a newspaper they started up and made bicycles from spare parts. When they finished school, the brothers supported themselves and their sister by running a bicycle shop where they built, repaired, and sold bicycles.

Flight had fascinated them ever since they were small boys, when their father gave them a helicopter-like toy that flew around the room. They also watched birds and wondered how birds flew. "We could not understand," Orville Wright later wrote, "that there was anything about a bird that would enable it to fly that could not be built on a larger scale and used by man."

It was while Orville was recovering from typhoid fever that the brothers discovered Lilienthal's work in a magazine article. Orville wasn't much of a reader, but with nothing to do while he lay in bed, he read and re-read the article on Lilienthal's work, building his own glider in his imagination. Wilbur was particularly fascinated by Lilienthal because the German inventor was one of the first who actually *practiced* gliding, instead of making one or two test glides as others had done. The brothers bought a copy of Lilienthal's book, *Experiments in Soaring,* and began work on their own gliders. They learned that Lilienthal and other experimenters in England and Europe were trying to control the gliders by shifting their bodies to balance the machines. The Wrights decided to find a better way. They set up a small wind tunnel to test glider models and in 1902 had developed improved designs for the wings and the elevators that kept the craft stable in the air. Tests of full-size gliders in the fields near Dayton and on the sands near Kitty Hawk, North Carolina, proved that their design, based more on box kites than on bird wings, was sound.

The next step was to give the machine power so that it could fly instead of merely glide. Their shop assistant, Charles Taylor, designed a gasoline-powered engine that was both light and powerful. The brothers designed a new propeller which was far more efficient than any propeller known at the time. By September of 1903, their flying machine was ready to test. They named it the *Flyer* and took it to Kitty Hawk to test. Unfortunately it was damaged in shipment. The first flight had to be delayed.

In December of 1903, Orville and Wilbur packed up the *Flyer* again and returned to Kitty Hawk on the 17th. A few local residents came out to watch and to assist with the trial. The brothers flipped a coin to see who would take the controls. Orville won. A bit nervously, he

Alpena County Library
211 N. First Ave.
Alpena, MI 49707

Daredevils of the Air

climbed into the craft and lay full length beside the engines, the primitive controls in his hands. Neither brother knew what would happen next, whether the craft would fly, or fail — or crash. Orville knew full well that Lilienthal and other inventors had been killed when their gliders had crashed. The *Flyer* was more than a glider. The propeller, mounted behind, was designed to push the craft through the air. A self-powered machine might fly faster than a glider. Orville hoped that the controls they had invented would actually work, or he was about to be in big trouble.

Wilbur started up the engine and the locals who were watching hung on to the ropes to hold the craft in place, as the *Flyer* had no brakes. At a signal from Orville, the helpers let go of the ropes. Driven by the spinning propeller, the *Flyer* slid along its skids down the sandy beach. Wilbur ran alongside. Orville pulled back on the control stick. The *Flyer* lifted a few yards off the ground. For twelve seconds it skimmed down the beach, finally landing 120 feet from where it had started. Orville Wright became the first person ever to fly a self-powered winged aircraft.

The brothers took turns flying their airplane three more times that day until the winds became too strong. Their fourth flight covered 852 feet. Visitors to Kitty Hawk today can see markers that show the distances the Wright Brothers flew on that day in December, 1903.

They telegraphed the news to their father back in Ohio, who promptly telegraphed the newspapers for miles around. Some papers printed the article, but many editors thought it was a joke and didn't bother with the story. The Wrights went back home to Ohio where they continued to

Thrilling Tales of Early Aviators

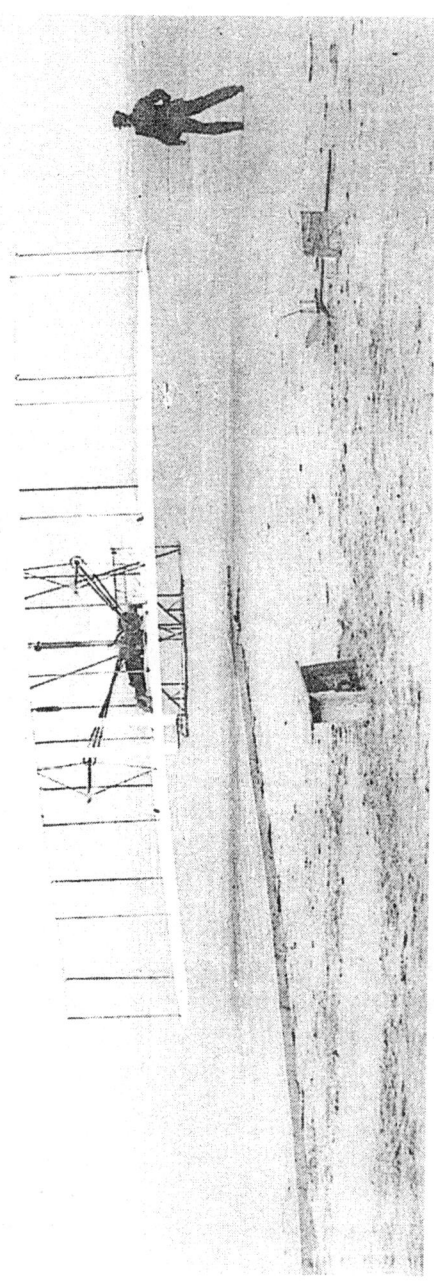

The historic first flight: on December 17, 1903, with Wilbur Wright at the helm, the Flyer left the ground for the first time, traveling only about 120 feet and staying up only about twelve seconds. But the world would never be the same.

experiment. The racket of their aircraft engine became a common sound around Dayton.

The only person in the U.S. who took serious notice of the Wright Brother's achievement was a motorcycle racer named Glenn Curtiss, who later became their chief competitor in the aircraft business. Frustrated by the cold reception their native country had given them, the Wright Brothers booked a trip to Europe, taking one of their airplanes with them. In 1908 the brothers gave flying demonstrations in France. Their flying machine electrified the French people, who had been experimenting with airplanes since Alberto Santos-Dumont had successfully built and tested a propeller-driven plane in 1906. The French believed Santos-Dumont had invented the world's first airplane. Not only had the Wright Brothers shattered the French record, their flying machine was far more graceful, elegant, and efficient than anything the French were flying at the time. Inspired by the Wrights' demonstrations, French aviators organized the world's first international flying exhibition in 1909 at Rheims, France.

The Wrights returned to the United States and gave public flight demonstrations. Americans by then had read rumors of working airplanes in America and stories about the first airshow in France, and they were hungry for a look at the incredible new machines. It was during one demonstration that the Orville Wright was involved in a crash that resulted in the first airplane fatality. At a demonstration at Fort Meyer, Orville took one of his planes up with a passenger, Lieutenant Thomas Selfridge. Selfridge was an associate of airman Glenn Curtiss. Curtiss had also been at a flight demonstration a few days before. In the middle of the flight, one of the propellers snapped, damaging a wing and sending the plane into a dive. Wright pulled back on the controls and took the plane up again, but the plane stalled and dropped into spin straight to the ground. Wright was dragged out of the wreckage, conscious but in pain from a broken thigh. Selfridge lay still, killed almost instantly by a blow to the head.

Despite a protracted court battle with Curtiss over their patented controls, a case that would occupy Orville's time and energy until the outbreak of World War I, the Wrights opened The Wright Company in New York in 1910. The company manufactured and improved airplanes as well as giving flying lessons, becoming the one of the country's first flight schools.

Wilbur Wright contracted typhoid fever and died in 1912. Orville continued running the company for several more years, then sold the rights to the company and retired in 1915.

Though Orville sent the original *Flyer* to the Science Museum in London. In 1948, shortly after Orville's death, the Science Museum gave the *Flyer* to the National Air and Space Museum in Washington, D.C., where it can be seen today.

Alberto Santos-Dumont, taken from a portriat at his family estate.

Chapter 2
A Brazilian in Paris
— Alberto Santos-Dumont

Though the Wright Brothers invented the first working airplane in Ohio, the capital of early aviation was Paris, France, ever since the very first hot-air balloon flight occurred nearby at the Palace of Versailles in 1783. While the U.S. almost ignored the Wright Brothers' achievement, French inventors were experimenting with gliders, balloons, and propeller-driven dirigibles. It was in Paris in 1906 that Brazilian-born Alberto Santos-Dumont, a resident of Paris, flew his airplane, the *14 bis*. For the next two years Parisians believed that one of their citizens had invented the first airplane, until the Wright Brothers gave their demonstrations in 1908.

Alberto Santos-Dumont was born on a coffee plantation in the province of Sao Paolo, Brazil, in 1873. From an early age he was fascinated by machinery. By seven he was steering a steam-powered tractor around the farm. At twelve, he was behind the controls of the plantation's railway engines. When he came of age he bought one of the first automobiles in Brazil. Yet it was machinery for soaring through the air that fascinated him most. Inspired by the fantastic novels of Jules Verne, young Santos-Dumont dreamed of taking to the air in machines such as the *Albatros*, an imaginary craft which appeared in Verne's novel *Robur the Conqueror*. When asked what he wanted to be when he grew up, Santos-Dumont often replied, to everyone's amusement, "A flying man."

When his father was badly injured in a fall from a horse while inspecting coffee machines, the family was forced to sell the plantation and move to France. Alberto was eighteen at the time. His father presented him with a fifth of the family's large fortune. With money to burn in Paris, Santos-Dumont soon realized his dreams of flying. Within a few years of arriving in France, Santos-Dumont bought his own balloon and took up the sport of balloon racing.

Santos-Dumont was in his element. Parisian life at the time glorified rich, young, eccentric dandies, and what could be more eccentric than floating over the French countryside in a balloon, sipping champagne and nibbling on *paté de fois gras*? The young Brazilian was so fascinated by aerial dining that he had the dining table in his home built six feet high. A servant had to climb on a step-stool to wait on the table.

Despite this dandyish beginning, Santos-Dumont was serious about flying. In 1898, no longer satisfied with just drifting along with the wind, he took up flying dirigibles. The invention of the gasoline engine and small steam engines meant that light, yet powerful engines could be fitted with propellers and taken aloft in balloons. So the first dirigibles were created, and young inventors were designing and racing the machines when Santos-Dumont came to Paris. Soon Santos-Dumont was designing his own dirigibles, creating fourteen new models which he flew over the city. One crash-landed in the Baroness de Rothschild's stylish garden and Santos-Dumont waited several hours, entangled in a chestnut tree, to be pulled down. As he and his aircraft dangled from the tree, an admirer arranged for a lunch to be taken up to him by ladder.

The setback only inspired Santos-Dumont to try even more daring stunts. In 1901, he entered a race to be the first to sail his airship from the Parisian suburb of Saint Cloud, around the Eiffel Tower, and back again in thirty minutes or less. After several tries, Santos-Dumont won the race and claimed a prize of 100,000 francs (about $20,000). The feat required not just a good engine capable of running the entire distance without overheating, but also an incredible amount of control to guide the craft down the course and back again regardless of the wind's speed and direction.

Sailing over Paris in a dirigible had its charms and had even proven profitable, but it still wasn't enough to satisfy Santos-Dumont. He read about Otto Lilienthal's gliders, and discovered some articles about new, better gliders and experiments with propellers by Orville and Wilbur Wright. When he watched another glider experimenter, Gabriel Voisin, soar over the Seine, Santos-Dumont was inspired. He borrowed the wing design used by Voisin and assembled a craft which he named the *14 bis*, a recognition of the fourteen dirigibles which he'd designed before it — *bis* means "encore" or "once again." To this machine he attached an engine with a propeller mounted in the back.

The *14 bis* was a strange-looking craft by today's standards. The wings looked like a half-dozen box-kites fastened together. The long body and the elevator stuck beak-like out in front. Two flimsy bicycle wheels were all the landing gear it had. The entire structure was built out of bamboo and canvas. Despite its ungainly appearance, Santos-Dumont believed it would fly.

On October 23, 1906, he took the *14 bis* to a field near Paris in a well-publicized attempt to fly it. He started up the engine and his assistants let go. Santos-Dumont stood in the cockpit, as the *14 bis* had no seat and was piloted from a standing position. The plane rolled along the field, gaining speed. At last it lifted three yards off the ground and soared for over 200 feet. Santos-Dumont had not designed an effective steering mechanism, and the flight turned quickly into an uncontrolled hop. The machine came down hard on the flimsy landing gear, crushing the undercarriage. Santos-Dumont escaped unhurt. The onlookers were ecstatic. Since word of the Wright Brothers' flight in 1903 had not reached Europe, everyone present believed they had just witnessed the first airplane flight.

Santos-Dumont went back to work on his craft, adding a stronger undercarriage and assembling primitive ailerons on the wings to provide some ability to steer and balance the craft. On the 12th of November, he took the *14 bis* into the air again for a flight distance of 722 feet. Soon after, he put away the craft and worked on other designs, including the world's first plywood airplane, a hydroplane which floated well but did not take off, and his favorite of all, the *Demoiselle*. In French, *demoiselle* means both "young girl" and "dragonfly." This little craft, constructed of bamboo and yellow Japanese silk — Santos-Dumont insisted on yellow for all his aircraft — was the first ultralight plane. The eight-meter-long craft could carry only one person, but it was the safest airplane available, could be partially broken down for transport by automobile, and was easy to fly.

When Englishman Lord Northcliffe heard of the flight of the *14 bis*, he was furious, imagining that, "England is no longer an island. There will be no sleeping safely behind the wooden walls of old England with the Channel our safety moat. It means the aerial chariots of a foe descending on British soil if war comes." Despite his initial fears, it was Lord Northcliffe who offered a large prize to the first aviator who could cross the English Channel in an airplane.

Northcliffe's predictions did eventually come true. Airplanes were first used for war in World War I, and German planes bombed London in the second World War. Santos-Dumont was horrified by the military use of airplanes and airships in the first World War and in his native Brazil. Depressed, ill with multiple sclerosis, and fearful for the future of aviation and the world in general, Santos-Dumont committed suicide in his home in Brazil in 1932.

Chapter 3
From June Bugs to Flying Boats
— Glenn Curtiss

Thomas Scott Baldwin was in serious trouble. A crowd waited in the hot afternoon sunshine to watch his airship, the *California Arrow*, take off and soar over Oakland, California, under its own power. The gas bag was filled and pushing against the tent that served as a hangar, but the engine that was supposed to turn the propeller refused to work. The men and women gathered had been there for two hours and had reached the end of their patience. Still the stubborn engine refused to give more than a few seconds of service before it coughed and quit.

As Baldwin primed the engine once more, he looked up and noticed something small and fast raising a cloud of dust on the nearby road. Whatever the thing was, the buzzing hum of its motor told Baldwin that here was a piece of machinery far superior to the one he was sweating and cursing over. He jumped down from his ship and sprinted over to the road.

The thing in the dust cloud resolved into a young man on a Hercules motorized bicycle. Baldwin flagged him down and asked to have a look at the machine. "Who makes them?" he wanted to know.

The youth gave him a name: Glenn H. Curtiss of Hammondsport, New York.

At the other end of the country, Glenn Curtiss was in

trouble. A California company threatened to sue him for using the name Hercules for his brand of motorized bicycle. The California firm had been using the name for their own motorized bicycles several years before Curtiss unknowingly adopted it. On the advice of his wife Lena, and his business partner Bill Damoth, Curtiss gave his company his own name and used his signature as a logo. His timing couldn't have been better. The Curtiss name was already far more famous than Glenn Curtiss had guessed, thanks to his many victories in motorcycle races, and motorcycles were just beginning to rise in popularity. Curtiss soon had more business that he could keep up with.

It was during this flood of orders that Curtiss' secretary handed him a letter from Baldwin. "Some nut from California wants you to build a motor for a balloon," she told him. Curtiss set it aside to think about. Six months later, Baldwin turned up in Hammondsport, along with his two mechanics Roy Knaubenshue and Lincoln Beachey, to ask how his engine was coming along.

Curtiss sheepishly admitted he hadn't even started yet. Fortunately, Baldwin was a good-humored man. Curtiss, Damoth, and the airmen examined the engine from the *California Arrow*. It was a heavy affair that overheated too quickly. Curtiss knew the engines of his motorbikes were cooled by the airstream of the speeding bike. The airship didn't get up enough speed to keep the engine cooled that way. By adjusting the propeller, he rigged a way for it to blow air on the engine, keeping the engine cool enough to operate. A few months later, Baldwin was back in California, successfully flying his airship with its new Curtiss engine.

Glenn Curtiss

Curtiss himself had no plans to get into the aviation business. He was too busy with his motorcycle company and with motorcycle racing. While Baldwin was sailing his airship in Oakland, Curtiss was designing what he hoped would be the fastest motorcycle in the world. The front wheel was large, the rear small, and the saddle was designed for the rider to lie almost flat. A heavy-duty frame was wrapped around a monstrous engine that ran like the devil for three minutes before overheating. But that was all Curtiss needed. In January of 1905, Curtiss started up his strange machine and roared down a one mile track at Ormond Beach in 26.4 seconds — 136.47 miles per hour. No one came anywhere close to the record for many years.

In the meantime, the success of the *California Arrow*

inspired would-be aviators from all over the world to write to the Curtiss company at Hammondsport asking for the same sort of engine that Baldwin had used. Baldwin himself returned to Hammondsport with an improved *California Arrow* and persuaded Curtiss to take a ride. Against the advice of his friends who were sure he'd break his neck, Curtiss agreed and took his first flight.

Curtiss felt none of the exhilaration that Baldwin had promised. The ride was interesting, but the airship bumbled along too sluggishly for the man who'd ridden the fastest motorized vehicle of any kind in the world.

The real beginning of Curtiss' aerial career came in 1906 when he was displaying his engines at the New York Aero Show. Dr. Alexander Graham Bell, the inventor of the telephone, was present. Bell was keenly interested in aeronautics, but felt that the future of flight was not in airships. He'd been experimenting with tetrahedral kites and had been reading about gliders, and felt sure that wings, not gasbags, would be the means of practical aviation. Bell was in search of light, powerful engines, and the innovative V-8 engine Curtiss had on display caught his attention.

Bell had been a good friend of Samuel Langley, whose ill-fated attempts to fly his *Aerodrome* had earned only derision. Bell had also heard rumors that two brothers named Wright had actually built a working airplane, though no one was sure. Curtiss was intrigued. The thought of building and flying a fast, winged craft was far more exciting than piloting a slow-moving airship.

Curtiss, Bell, and a few other enthusiasts formed the Aerial Experiment Association, which was eventually headquartered in Curtiss' engine factory. By 1908, after a great deal of experimentation with man-lifting kites and glider models, the Association constructed its first aircraft. The machine was covered in red silk, so they dubbed it the *Red Wing*. On March 12, 1908, the *Red Wing* made its first flight across the ice of Lake Keuka, traveling a total distance of 318 feet. The *Red Wing* crashed on a second flight and was a total loss.

Next came the *White Wing*. Curtiss designed a way to change the shape of the wing tips to give greater control than the *Red Wing* had. Curtiss himself piloted the *White Wing* 1017 feet on May 22 of 1908. But the wing tips were too flexible, and the *White Wing* crashed on several of its flights until finally it was broken beyond repair.

Curtiss went back to modeling new designs. Knowing the importance of understanding the flow of air over a wing, he created a box-shaped wind tunnel for testing his models. He invented a new design for the wing flaps, creating the first real ailerons. The machine Curtiss built based on his new design was painted with yellow varnish and taken to a field outside Hammondsport. Curtiss took it up in the air and found it flew more smoothly than the prior two machines. Then suddenly the plane shot upward, out of control. Curtiss cut the engine and managed a safe landing, then tried again. At the same spot over the landscape he hit the same updraft, and this time rode it higher than he'd ever flown. He gently guided the airplane over a vineyard until he found an open field, then took it down, 1,266 feet from his takeoff point. Bell, who'd been watching, said the machine flew like a June Bug, and that's what they named the craft.

While Curtiss was learning to handle the *June Bug*, the Aero Club of America, normally an extremely conservative organization of balloon pilots, surprised the nation by announcing a radically new contest: The *Scientific American* Cup for feats of heavier-than-air-craft flight. The first cup was offered for an airplane that could fly a distance of at least one kilometer. On July 4, 1908, representatives of the Aero Club came reluctantly to Hammondsport. They'd heard rumors of Curtiss and his Association somewhere out in the sticks, and wondered openly if they were off to see a bunch of crackpots. Curtiss had the *June Bug* oiled, polished, and ready for them.

Curtiss started the engine and scrambled into the seat. He took the *June Bug* into the air, but a rear stabilizer was out of place and the whole tail drooped. Curtiss dropped to a landing as quickly as possible and his fellow aviators quickly repaired the machine while the Aero Club men snickered. A few hours later Curtiss fired the craft up again and jumped back in the pilot's seat. The *June Bug* smoked and roared. Curtiss rose into the air and guided the machine down the course. He passed the half-mile mark, banked gracefully to avoid rough country, and put the *June Bug* down just a few feet short of a red flag that marked a full mile. He'd flown well over the kilometer distance required for the cup.

Unfortunately for Curtiss, the Wright Brothers had been paying close attention to his accomplishments and sent notice that they intended to sue over violation of one of their patents. Orville Wright claimed his patent covered any type of adjustable wing surface that changed the angle of attack on the wing, allowing for changes of direction and speed. Curtiss and Bell disagreed, believing that the Wright patent only covered the Wrights' flexible wing-warping design, not Curtiss' movable ailerons which were part of a rigid wing. Curtiss and the Wrights would wrangle for years over the suit, until the outbreak of World War I brought the need for aircraft innovation from anyone who could deliver it.

In 1909, the Aero Club of New York asked Curtiss to enter the first international air meet in Rhiems, France and offered to pay his expenses. The president of the Aero club had first approached the Wright Brothers, but they were interested only in the science of flight and felt that air races and dangerous stunt flying would only impede the progress of aviation by convincing the public that flying was dangerous and best left to professionals. Curtiss, too, shared their views, and also felt that he wasn't a good enough pilot to compete. His friends, however, urged him to give it a try, and a patriotic appeal from the president of the Aero Club finally convinced him.

Curtiss and his team built the *Golden Flyer*, forever known afterwards as the "Rhiems Machine." It was powered by a V-8 water-cooled engine, the most powerful aircraft engine Curtiss had designed. He packed up the plane and his team and boarded a steamer to France. In Rheims, Curtiss felt humbled by the great European flyers with their tailored costumes and their sleek machines. He knew he was outclassed in most of the events, and set his sights at winning just one: the *Coupe Internationale d'Aviation*, a distance race. While the European flyers were eager to get into the air regardless of the weather, Curtiss bided his time. He watched Hubert Latham win the *Prix d'Altitiude* for flying to a height of 503.79 feet, and Eugene Lefébre take the Gordon Bennett prize for flying two miles in 19 minutes and 24 seconds.

Finally, knowing he needed practice in his new plane, Curtiss entered the daily *Tour de Piste*, a short speed trial of one lap around a ten kilometer course. On his first trial, Curtiss roared around the pylons in 8 minutes, 35 seconds, breaking all previous records. The next day his record was broken by Louis Blériot, the French aviator who had flown the English Channel just one month before.

The *Golden Flyer* developed engine problems. Curtiss and his team tore the engine apart and overhauled it completely. As they worked, Curtiss thought. He'd watched his competitors fly and knew their planes were as fast as his or faster. To win any of the races, he had to find some other means than just speed to give him the edge.

Finally it came to him. He'd entered a cross-country motorcycle race years before and when he inspected the course, he found a sharp turn in the road which he knew would slow everyone down. On the day of the race, while other riders were slowing down for the curve, Curtiss raced his engine and sped straight at it. He rode up onto the steep bank and shot around the curve, making what was probably the first banked turn in the history of motorcycle racing. If he could apply the same principle to the air race, he might have an edge there as well.

Curtiss announced to everyone's surprise that he was starting the *Coupe Internationale* right then and there. He fired up his plane and rumbled out to the course, ready to fly the two laps for a distance of 20 kilometers. As he reached the first pylon, he took the plane up slightly, then turned it on its side and dove around the corner, leveling off just above the ground. The crowd gasped, thinking his plane was out of control. Only when he repeated the maneuver on the second pylon did they realize the sideways dive was a deliberate, daring move. The little golden plane screamed around the course a second time, diving at each pylon, and crossing the finish line at a remarkable 15 minutes, 50.4 seconds, for an average speed of 47.65 miles per hour. His team held their collective breaths as Louis Blériot, clearly worried, drove his big monoplane hard down the course. But the French flyer was 5 1/2 seconds short. Curtiss had won the silver cup and the $5000 purse that went with it.

Curtiss flew in other events in the Unites States to raise money, but disliked exhibition flying. It was easy money, but the publicity felt cheap and he hated to leave his serious work. Besides, too many young pilots were performing daring stunts and getting themselves killed, and people were crowding to airshows for the morbid thrill of seeing pilots die. Still he needed the money, and established the Curtiss Exhibition Team to do the actual flying while he got back to work. One of his most dashing and popular pilots was Lincoln Beachey, one of Thomas Baldwin's former mechanics.

Curtiss began went back to working on another innovation that would eventually secure his place in aviation history. The land around Hammondsport was pockmarked with tiny lakes, and Curtiss knew there were similar lakes and broad rivers all over the country. Thinking into the future of long-distance flight, Curtiss realized that in many parts of the country, flat fields for safe landing were few, while rivers and lakes were abundant. If he could invent an aircraft that could take off from and land on water, his crafts could be the means of reaching even the wildest country by air. He'd experimented with putting pontoons on a plane before, but had only achieved marginal success.

Frustrated by his inability to work on frozen lake Keuka several months out of the year, he established winter quarters in San Diego and soon solved the problem of float planes. By cutting away the lower rear portion of the pontoon, he created the hydroplane step, an innovation that helped float planes break free of the surface of the water.

With this success, Curtiss worked actively to interest the Navy in aviation. One of his pilots took off from a steep wooden ramp on the deck of a battleship and later landed a plane on a ship, demonstrating the possibilities of building an aircraft carrier. Curtiss himself flew a float plane to the side of a battleship where it was hoisted onto the ship, and later lowered for takeoff. The Navy was convinced, and contracted with Curtiss to build his new design, the flying boats.

Curtiss built a small flying boat, the *America*, intending to fly it across the Atlantic, but the outbreak of the first World War ended his plans. The Curtiss company went to war as well, supplying the U.S. Armed forces with the JN series of biplanes, known affectionately as "Jennies." The Jenny would later earn fame as a favorite plane of the barnstormers.

In 1919, after the war, the Navy asked Curtiss to build four flying boats, the Navy-Curtiss or NC series, dubbed "Nancies." The NC-2 was damaged in a fire, but the NC-1, NC-3, and NC-4 were flown to Trepassy Bay in Newfoundland. With Naval vessels posted across their watery route to help guide the way, the three flying boats took off from the bay and headed east across the Atlantic. Fog obscured their view and the crews were flying blind for much of the route. The NC-1 was forced down into the Atlantic and the crew was rescued by a destroyer. The NC-3 was also forced down and damaged. The crew sailed the stricken plane, which lived up to its name as a flying *boat*, all the way to the Azores Islands. The NC-4, commanded by Lieutenant Commander Albert Read, reached the Azores safely, then flew on to Lisbon in Portugal. Read and his crew became the first to fly across the Atlantic Ocean, eight years before Charles Lindbergh's solo flight in 1927.

Chapter 4
The Master Birdman
— Lincoln Beachey

In June of 1905, the residents of Washington D.C. heard a clattering roar in the skies and looked up to see a crude, home-built dirigible slowly circling the Washington Monument. The little airship cruised toward the White House where it settled down on the lawn. A dapper young pilot, only eighteen years old, jumped out of the craft and announced that he had come to visit President Roosevelt. The president wasn't at home, but Mrs. Roosevelt came out and was introduced to the audacious pilot, Lincoln Beachey.

Beachey, know to his friends as "Link," was born in San Francisco in 1887. At the age of 13 he showed his characteristically cocky independence when he opened his own bicycle shop, where two years later he was busy repairing motorcycles and their engines. Then balloons caught his fancy and Beachey began hanging around exhibition grounds whenever balloons and airships came to town. He built his own balloon, learned to fly it, and started putting on exhibitions himself. This caught the attention of Thomas Baldwin, a balloon pilot. Baldwin liked Beachey's energy and dash, and hired him as a mechanic and performer.

Baldwin wanted to build a dirigible, and Beachey was to help him. Together they planned and constructed the *California Arrow*. When the engine failed to perform,

Baldwin took Beachey and another mechanic, Roy Knaubenshue, to New York State where they met motorcycle builder Glenn Curtiss and worked with him to build a new engine for the dirigible. Curtiss' engine was a success, and Baldwin went on to fly the *California Arrow* over San Francisco Bay in 1904 and at the St. Louis World's Fair later in the same year.

Beachey himself piloted an airship for the first time in 1905, and decided he might build his own dirigible. He left Baldwin's company and traveled to Toledo, where he joined up with Knaubenshue. There they bought yards of silk for the gas bag and cut it to pieces in the upper story of a street car barn. After hiring a seamstress to sew it up, Beachey built a wooden gondola and wove a net to hold the bag in place and suspend the gondola beneath it. He made his first exhibition of the dirigible over Pittsburgh's Luna Park in 1906.

But Beachey wanted to make a bigger splash to make his business an immediate success. That inspired the idea to pack his "Rubber Cow" off to Washington, D.C, where he paid his famous call on the White House. The stunt earned him all the publicity he wanted. The daring young pilot was a sensation, and before long he was booked at airshows all over the country.

His success with dirigibles and balloons lasted until 1910, when Beachey attended an international air show in Los Angeles. There Beachey got his first look at an airplane, flown by a French pilot, Henri Farman. When Beachey raced his dirigible around a course against the speedy airplane, he was soundly beaten. "Boy, our racket is dead!" he said to a friend, and indeed it was. Even as early as 1910, the American public was growing tired of

Lincoln Beachey, who combined flying skill, aerial stunts, and sheer danger to help popularize aviation.

slow airships and was entranced with graceful, darting airplanes. Beachey promptly gave up airships and went east to find Curtiss again. By that time Curtiss was building airplanes, and Beachey intended to have one.

Beachey enrolled in the Curtiss Flying School. On his first solo flight, Beachey took a plane almost straight up, stalled it, and dropped it tail-first, smashing the craft to pieces. Incredibly, he walked away with barely a scratch while Curtiss turned away in disbelief. His second solo ended in another crash. Curtiss was furious and threatened to turn Beachey away. Yet he gave the would-be airplane pilot another chance, and on his third try, Beachey successfully soloed in a pusher biplane. When Curtiss hired Beachey as part of his exhibition team, he was glad he'd given the young man a third chance, for Beachey became the team's most popular performer by far. He was everything the audiences wanted: young, handsome, fearless. While most pilots donned leather helmets and flying gear, Beachey went stylish in a black suit, diamond stickpin, and oversized checkered golf cap turned backwards to keep it from flying off.

Beachey was more than daring — he was unstoppable. He flew at airshows all across the country, thrilling audiences with his trademark "death dip." After taking the plane up to 5000 feet, Beachey hurtled down from the skies, hands off the controls and arms outstretched, dropping so fast the audience could hear the wind whistling through the reinforcing wires. At the last minute he would level off and skim across the ground, his hands still out to his sides. Some early biplanes were controlled by lines attached to a yoke which strapped around the pilot's body, a foot bar connected to the rudder, and a stick that controlled the elevator. Most pilots who watched Beachey knew how to handle the yoke controls, but no one guessed he was gripping the stick with his knees. The few who imitated him plunged to their deaths, and Beachey, feeling responsible, later gave up the stunt.

He had plenty of other tricks up his immaculate sleeve, however. In fact, Beachey's repertoire of aerobatics was probably larger than any other pilot's in that day. No wonder, then, that the newspapers called him "The Master Birdman."

Only six months after learning to fly, Beachey performed what would be his most memorable stunt of all — a flight through Niagara Falls. A crowd of 150,000 gathered on the riverbanks below the falls to watch the Master Birdman risk his life. Beachey began with a swoop over lower Niagara Falls, then flew to the Canadian side,

2000 feet upstream. He came soaring down the river, circled twice at the brink of the American Falls, then tipped over the brink and plunged down the falls. The crowd screamed as he disappeared into the spray. A few moments later Beachey and his plane emerged, dripping wet, skimming a few feet above the water. But he wasn't done yet. Straight ahead was a suspension bridge between the U.S. and Canadian sides of the river, and beneath it a gap only 168 feet wide and 100 feet high. Beachey raced the engine and sped straight through the opening under the bridge, then roared up the narrow gorge of the cataract with the engine wide open. He nosed the plane up toward the Canadian shore, the engine coughing and sputtering, and barely cleared the cliff's edge with only a few feet to spare. He later called this the most thrilling feat of his career, but he never tried it again.

Beachey didn't fly only for the thrills and the money, though the money he earned was considerable and helped the Curtiss company immensely. He was also a serious pilot and put his mind to solving many of the problems of controlling the delicate planes of his time. His greatest contribution came when he figured out how to conquer the spin. Many pilots had been killed when they lost control and their planes went into a spin, straight into the ground. Beachey figured there must be a solution. One morning in 1911 he took his plane up to 5000 feet, nosed it over, and deliberately forced it into a spin. He kicked the rudder control at his feet hard in the direction of the spiral. The plane slowly responded, and by opening up the engine and applying more power, Beachey pulled it level. Thinking perhaps it was only luck, he tried the maneuver again. Once more, a strong shove on the rudder in the direction of the spin pulled him out and he regained control. Beachey continued studying other accidents, analyzing the sequence of events and trying to figure out a way the accident could have been prevented. A few months after his Niagara adventure, Beachey entered the Chicago International Aviation Meet of 1911. Conditions were far from perfect, and the pilots grumbled openly when it became apparent that the judges, who were not flyers, did not understand the dangers that Chicago's capricious winds held for the fragile aircraft. The judges held races at the posted times regardless of the weather, saying that the flyers understood the conditions and could judge for themselves whether they should fly or not. The pilots did understand the conditions — and flew in spite of them, preferring to risk their necks than than lose their reputations. Two pilots, Harold McCormick and William Badger, took the chance and lost their lives.

Beachey took the risks and won again and again. He flew in nearly every event and racked up ten awards, including speed races for biplanes in which he employed Glenn Curtiss' diving turn technique around the pylons. He took the lead in an eight mile race when his fiercest competitor, Earle Ovington, hit a pylon and was disqualified. The same day Beachey filled the fuel tank of his little Curtiss biplane, took it straight up until it ran out of fuel at a record 7,917 feet. He nosed the plane over and glided downward again to a perfect dead-stick landing. The next day he won a twelve mile race, though his time was a few seconds short of the record set by Ovington the prior day. When his altitude record was beaten by two other pilots, Beachey insulated himself with heavy wool clothes, filled the tanks again, and flew up for an hour and forty-eight minutes until his fuel was gone and the engine sputtered and died. The plane dropped in a series of graceful spirals, and Beachey guided it to a gentle landing in front of the hangar. He was numb and stiff with cold as he crawled out of the machine and staggered off to meet Curtiss. The barograph attached to the plane showed he'd reached a freezing 11,578 feet, a new world's record.

The meet was extended one more day to raise money for McCormick's young widow, but the winds were fierce all day, keeping the pilots grounded. Even Beachey gave up after one circle of the field. By the evening the crowd began demanding its money's worth and something had to be done. Wright team pilot Cal Rodgers lit up his trademark cigar, climbed into his biplane, and shouted, "Let 'er go!" Beachey soon followed, giving his wildest performance of the entire meet. As he rolled, spiraled, and swooped in the gale-force winds, Glenn Curtiss shook his head and remarked, "Two months ago we would have thought a man crazy or trying to commit suicide who went up in air like this." Both pilots performed the death-defying spiral-and-dip, but while Rodgers kept his plane low, Beachey flew up to a thousand feet, then came whirling downward, turning circles around Rodgers' machine and sailing in an arch over top of him. The audience was satisfied, and the gate receipts totaled over $10,000 for the benefit of Mrs. McCormick.

Any place a crowd could be scraped together, Beachey would fly. In 1913, he was hired to perform at the San Francisco World's Fair. There he took off inside the immense Machinery Hall, where he took the plane up to a speed of 60 miles per hour to the crowd's astonishment. When he landed, he hit a wet spot on the smooth floor and his plane careened out of control and crashed into wall. Beachey walked away unhurt.

In the same year, Beachey learned that a French pilot had mastered the art of flying a loop. Beachey, who hated being bested at anything, went to Curtiss and asked for a plane that could fly a loop. Curtiss refused. Beachey stormed off in a rage and declared his retirement from the flying business. It wasn't only Curtiss' refusal that drove him away. He was also disgusted with what he felt was the real reason audiences gathered to watch him fly. "I am convinced that the only thing that draws crowds is the morbid desire to see something happen," he said. "They call me the 'Master Birdman,' but they pay to see me die."

And he was right. Sadly, though European nations offered prizes for long distance flights and progressive accomplishments in aviation, the only way for a pilot to make money in the United States was by performing death-defying dives and stunts for a paying audience which howled for more and more thrills.

Beachey tried the real estate business in San Francisco for a short time, but his heart wasn't in it. Reluctantly, Curtiss built him a new plane capable of turning loops. While taking the little aerobatic plane out for the first time, Beachey had his first real brush with death. Two young women were watching from the roof of a Navy hangar at Hammondsport when Beachey was learning to turn loops. He misjudged his speed coming out of the loop and accidentally struck the women. Ruth Hildreth was killed instantly and her sister was rushed to the hospital in critical condition. Beachey himself was severely injured and lay in the hospital, deeply depressed, wondering what to do with himself. Two ideas came to him. One was a suggestion to Glenn Curtiss to try rebuilding Samuel Langley's *Aerodrome* to see if the machine really could fly as Beachey suspected it could, a suggestion which Curtiss successfully followed up on. The second was inspired by a poster his manager plastered on his bedroom wall: a picture of Beachey flying upside-down, a feat he'd yet to accomplish. Soon he was on a train to San Diego for yet another airshow.

At the San Diego Exhibition in November of 1913, Beachey saw two Army pilots killed in crashes of their outdated planes. Furious, he fired telegrams off to the Secretary of War and the Secretary of the Navy, offering to come to Washington D.C. and show them the harm they were doing by forcing their pilots to fly in unsafe aircraft. Later he would take a poke the Army again in a monograph titled *The Genius of Aviation* which promoted aviation progress, but that afternoon he surprised his audience by performing high-altitude loops for the first time in the country.

Beachey perfected his loops, but soon discovered they were a financial wash-out. No one would pay to see a maneuver which they could view from outside the gates for free. He had to have another gimmick, and his manager soon came up with a sure-fire hit. He hired race car driver Barney Oldfield, built a high fence around the airfield to screen the view from casual onlookers, and had Beachey in his plane race Oldfield in his car around a track. They took turns winning and the audience was thrilled at the combination of daredevils of both earth and sky in the same arena. Together, Beachey and Oldfield made a quarter of a million dollars in their first year.

In the meantime, Beachey continued looping. Every

time he read about French pilots making record numbers of loops, he would set out to beat them, until he was doing eighty loops in a single afternoon. He had a new plane built which he called "The Little Looper." It was a speedy little machine powered by a French-built *Gnôme* rotary motor. Beachey's name was painted on the upper surface of the wings for all to see when he was at the peak of his loop.

Beachey staged another audience-thrilling act at the opening of the Panama-Pacific Exhibition in San Francisco on New Year's Day of 1915. Onlookers gasped in horror when they saw Beachey blow up the battleship *Oregon* and its crew — or so it appeared. His target was actually a wooden effigy anchored a mile offshore, but there were 100 genuine sailors aboard who helped run the realistic pyrotechnics. A tugboat took them away before they were in any real danger. The crowd of 80,000 was in a panic, believing he'd actually destroyed the battleship and had killed hundreds of sailors. Beachey walked off with half the gate receipts.

Though Beachey mastered death-defying maneuvers and conquered the spin, he couldn't defy death forever. On Sunday, March 15, 1915, Beachey flew out over San Francisco Bay in a sleek, black aerobatic monoplane newly built for him by Warren Eaton. He'd made three test flights in it already, and was ready to perform for an audience of 50,000 people. He hoped to make the first public demonstration of upside-down flight. He completed a loop, then turned the plane over for his inverted flight. He'd misjudged his altitude, however, and at 2000 feet there wasn't enough height for him to complete the maneuver. He yanked the controls, trying to pull his plane over and out of its sinking path. The strain was too much for the little monoplane. First the left wing snapped, then the right, and the fuselage plunged in a screaming dive straight into the bay.

Ironically, it was the crew of the real battleship *Oregon* who dove down in thirty feet of water to pull what was left of the monoplane out of the mud where it was embedded. Beachey was still firmly strapped in the seat, probably killed instantly by the impact.

Beachey's death inspired newspaper editors to protest against stunt flying. They wrote of their hopes that people would turn away in disgust from the morbid spectacle of stunt flying with its high death toll, and support real progress in aviation. The most far-seeing editors dreamed of a day when flying would be safe form of transportation for all. At the time, it was daring pilots like Beachey who promoted aviation progress in America, and each step forward was paid for dearly in human life.

Louis Blériot

Chapter 5
The Race Across the English Channel
— Louis Blériot and Hubert Latham

Un homme du monde," was how French pilot Hubert Latham described himself — "a man of the world." Handsome, cool, with a carefully cultivated image of the ultimate in French sophistication, Latham came from a family of wealthy, English-born ship owners in LeHavre. He had indulged himself of the usual pastimes of gentlemen of his era — lion hunting in Africa, automobile racing, exploration of Indo-China — and took an interest in the latest fashionable sport, heavier-than-air aviation. In 1909, Latham bought a French-built Antoinette monoplane, thought by many to be one of the most graceful designs. Within a few months, Latham was setting records for speed and duration, becoming an overnight sensation.

In the same year, Lord Northcliffe of England offered a prize to the first pilot who could cross the English Channel by airplane. Northcliffe owned the English newspaper, the *Daily Mail*, and used it to advertise his offer. Latham decided to make a try for it.

For sheer distance and time aloft, it would hardly be record-breaking. Other pilots had already flown greater distances cross-country and had set longer records of time in the air. Crossing the Channel itself, however, was remarkable for the dangers involved. Pilots would have no safe landing place. The Channel was often obscured by fog and prone to vile weather. And in the early days of flying, before sophisticated navigation devices, the lack of any landmarks for navigation over the open waters was a serious handicap.

Furthermore, crossing the Channel by air would have a powerful psychological effect. For centuries, England had relied on the Channel to help protect its lands from invasion. Only the bravest and best-equipped forces attempted to invade the British Isles by crossing the foggy, storm-tossed waters of the Channel. But if the distance could be crossed in less than an hour by air, England could no longer sit complacently behind her moat. Though Northcliffe had offered the prize, he feared the consequences of anyone winning.

In July of 1909, Latham arrived with his crew and his plane in Calais, France, where the distance from France to England would be the shortest. Unfortunately, summer rains had set in, and by July 12, Calais was a sea of mud. The local residents, however, were unfailingly enthusiastic.

On July 19, when the winds finally subsided, Latham took off from the top of a cliff at Sangatte. The Antoinette dove into the fog and quickly disappeared from view. Latham was seven miles out when he prepared to take an aerial photo of the torpedo-boat *Harpon* that had been assigned to follow him. As he aimed the camera, the engine of the Antoinette sputtered and died. Latham tried to restart it but the damp air was too much. All he could do was guide the plane down to the surface of the Channel, becoming the first pilot to make a successful water landing. The crew of the *Harpon* found him moments later, calmly smoking a cigarette and looking nonchalant as he waited in the floating monoplane. After he and his plane were fished out of the water, Latham declared he would try again.

But before Latham could get in the air again he faced another contender. Dark, solid, with a hawk-like nose and drooping moustache, Louis Blériot was quintessentially French. He had been trained as an engineer at one of France's leading technical schools. His income, a large one of 60,000 francs a year, came from his business of manufacturing and selling automobile headlights and accessories, supported by the growing auto craze in France. Since 1900, Blériot had been experimenting with aircraft of various sorts. All had one thing in common — they did not fly. One bizarre model had tubular wings fore and aft. Another resembled Otto Lilienthal's early gliders. Finally in 1907, Blériot constructed the *Blériot VI*, which took to the air. Despite many crashes, Blériot continued building and testing various aircraft.

Blériot made the first round-trip cross country flight from Goury to Artenay and back again, a distance of 28 km. In July of 1909, he flew from Etampes to Orléans, 42 km, in 45 minutes, which won the Aéro-Club de France's *Prix du Voyage* of 14,000 francs. After this he decided he was ready to try for the Northcliffe prize.

His only problem was that Latham was already camped out on the Channel coast. An even more serious complication was that Blériot was on crutches owing to severe burns he'd suffered in a recent crash. Blériot decided to wait, and on July 19, he heard the news that Latham had been forced to ditch in the Channel. Blériot immediately notified the *Daily Mail* that he intended to try for the prize.

Blériot quickly set up camp near the cliffs of Sangatte. He hoped that with luck he would be able to get into the air before Latham repaired his Antoinette. When Latham heard that Blériot had arrived, his crews worked night and day. By the 23rd of July, the Antoinette was ready, but gale-force winds kept both pilots on the ground.

At 2:00 on the morning of July 25, Blériot's associate, Alfred LeBlanc, woke up and saw that the winds had calmed. He rushed to the hotel where Blériot was staying and woke the pilot, urging him to take off as soon as he could. Blériot was hesitant at first, as was his wife, but a brief warm-up flight convinced him it was time to try.

Latham's crew was keeping a close eye on Blériot and saw the warm up-flights. Blériot had to wait for sunrise according to the rules of the *Daily Mail* prize, and Latham's crew thought Blériot was only making a test flight. But when at sunrise Blériot soared over Les Barques, just south of Calais, then aimed his plane at the Channel and headed west over the water, they realized the pilot was indeed underway. At the news, Latham rushed to the beach, but Blériot was already disappearing in the mist. Latham watched with tears in his eyes as his chance at the prize flew out of sight.

Thirty-six and a half exhausting minutes later, after battling high winds, down-drafts, and an engine that was prone to overheating, Blériot reached the English side of the Channel. It was hardly the greatest feat of navigation made by a pilot. Blériot had flown off-course and reached the English coastline well north of his destination. He laboriously turned the plane around and followed the coast south, and finally found his landing site where one of his crew was enthusiastically waving a French flag.

Blériot's landing at Dover Castle was really a crash, as he fell almost straight down from a height of 60 feet, breaking the undercarriage and one of the propeller blades. Yet he had succeeded, by determination and luck, before either the English or the Americans. France went wild. The song on everyone's lips was:

> *Blériot, c'est notoire*
> *En quittant Callais*
> *Entra dans l'Histoire*
> *Sans sceptre ou palais.*

> Blériot, it's no mystery
> When leaving Calais
> Became a part of History
> Without a scepter or a palace.

Chapter 6
Across America, Crash by Crash
— Cal Rodgers

In 1911, William Randolph Hearst offered a $50,000 prize to the first person who could fly an airplane across the United States in thirty days or less. Few people thought it possible. Nevertheless, three pilots decided to try the impossible for the chance at a sum of money that was a small fortune in those days.

The major contenders for the Hearst prize were Robert Fowler, who was starting from California, and an ex-jockey named Jimmy Ward who took off from New York. Both men were already in the air when a third pilot decided to try his luck. Calbraith Perry Rodgers — just plain "Cal" to his friends — had learned to fly just that year at the Wright Brothers' school, but had already won awards flying for the Wright team in the Chicago International Air Meet and figured he had as good a chance as any.

Rodgers demonstrated much of the same blend of dignity and determination shown by his great-grandfather, Commodore Matthew Calbraith Perry, who served in the United States Navy in the War of 1812 and the Mexican War. Commodore Perry also led a naval mission to Japan to negotiate treaties and begin trade agreements — aided by an impressive and intimidating display of gunboats off of Japan's shores. Rodgers' father was an Army captain who served in the Wyoming and Dakota territories. In August of 1878, Captain Rodgers was caught out on the plains in a thunderstorm and was killed by a bolt of lightning. Cal Rodgers was born a few months later, on January 12, 1879.

Maria Rodgers, Cal's mother, moved in with her mother in Pittsburgh. In a sleepy suburb of the Pennsylvanian city, young Cal grew up as a serious child who loved to tinker with anything mechanical but didn't care much for books. A bout with scarlet fever at the age of six left him partially deaf, which may have contributed to his preference for sports over the schoolroom where hearing his lessons was a problem. He excelled on the playing field in just about any sport he took up. At eighteen, Rodgers enrolled in Mercersburg Academy, a preparatory school headed by William Irvine. There he joined clubs by the handful and played at every sport he could manage. At 6 feet 3 inches, he was the tallest man on his football team.

After graduation, Rodgers moved to New York to be near his married sister. He joined the New York Yacht Club, which gave him not only the advantage of a good social circle, but also a uptown address at an affordable price. It was at a yachting event that Rodgers saw a pretty young woman accidentally fall into the water. Rodgers dove in and rescued her. The woman's name was Mabel Graves, and the rescue must have made a favorable impression on her, because on May 4, 1906, Mabel Graves became Mrs. Cal Rodgers.

Soon after his marriage, Rodgers moved away from New York and gave up yachting. He took up automobiling and motorcycle riding with enthusiasm. But in 1911, Rodgers took up a new hobby, one in which he would make history. His cousin John Rodgers, an Army

Daredevils of the Air

officer, had been assigned to the Wright Brothers' flying school to learn to fly. John wrote to Cal about the thrills of flying: "There's nothing like it. You're up there, watching the land glide by, bobbing, dipping as if in a boat, but you can see nothing, only feel it. For speed, you can't beat flying."

Cal Rodgers couldn't resist. He arrived in Dayton, Ohio in June of 1911 and plunked down $850 to learn to fly.

Lessons began on a balancing machine, a mock-up of a Wright plane. In essence, it was an early flight simulator. Students learned to operate the controls using the machine, and learned how to use the patented wing-warping feature which controlled the plane by bending the wings and moving the rudder at the same time. Controls

Cal Rodgers (facing) making a pre-flight check. A fearless flier, his many crashes finally ended with his own death.

were operated by a vertical lever between the two seats. Pushing the stick forward raised the right wing and depressed the left, causing the plane to bank left. Pulling it backwards made the plane bank right. A hinged handle at the top allowed for sharper control. A second vertical lever on the outer side of the pilot's seat controlled the elevators. When pushed forward, the plane nosed down. Drawing the lever back raised the plane up. Most pilots learned to fly from either the right or the left seat, but not both.

When he was not practicing on the balancing machine, Rodgers spent time with Charles Taylor, the mechanic who built the engine for the first Wright *Flyer*. There Rodgers learned about how the Wright engines worked.

When he was ready for the air, Rodgers worked with Arthur Welsh, a Wright flight instructor. The plane had dual controls, and Rodgers learned at first by putting his hands on the controls while Welsh moved them. On his third lesson he mastered banked turns. On his fourth, he took control of the plane during most of the flight. Rodgers learned to glide with the engine off, an important skill if the fuel ran out. Also, at that time, planes were landed with the engine off since they had no brakes. When ready for his solo flight, Rodgers ordered a Wright Model B of his own. He passed his tests for a pilot's license on August 7, 1911.

No sooner did he have his "wings" than Rodgers began exhibition flying. He decided to enter the Chicago International Aviation Meet in August of 1911. The meet gave Chicago residents and visitors thrills galore. One citizen was seen hanging out of a taxi window to watch several biplanes soar by. When the driver warned him that he might miss his train if they didn't get moving, the man replied, "I don't care. I've lived to be sixty years old without ever having seen anything like this, and I guess I will have to miss the train." Many of the aviators came close to disaster in the brisk Chicago winds. Two planes fell into Lake Michigan and one was burned when it became entangled with electrical wires, but all three pilots survived. Three other pilots, however, were killed in crashes. The meet was extended a day to raise money for the widow of one pilot. Rodgers and Curtiss pilot Lincoln Beachey flew exhibitions on the final day in spite of high winds.

Rodgers walked away at the end of the exhibition with a handful of prizes and an even greater hunger for flight. He had been pondering the Hearst challenge ever since he finished flight school, and decided it was time to try.

Rodgers knew he would need cash to complete the journey, which promised to be expensive. The Armor company offered to sponsor his flight if he would advertise their new grape-flavored soft drink, Vin Fiz. Rodgers painted the soft drink's name on his Wright biplane and christened it the *Vin Fiz Flyer*. He even fastened a bottle of the syrup on one of the front struts of his plane.

With a corporate sponsor paying him all expenses plus five dollars for every mile he flew east of the Mississippi and four dollars for each mile west, Rodgers was able to hire a special train to follow him and to carry a crew, spare parts, his wife and his mother. One car was painted bright white so that he could spot the train easily from the air. Among his crew was Charles Taylor, the Wright Brothers' mechanic.

On September 17, 1911, Rodgers took off from Sheepshead Bay, New York, announcing that he wouldn't quit until he wet his wheels in the Pacific Ocean. The only instrument he had was a piece of string nailed to one strut as a primitive bank indicator. Rodgers didn't even have a compass to guide him, relying on the landscape below him for navigation, as well as the distinctive railcar. He intended to follow the railway lines as he crossed the country.

Rodgers flew into New Jersey to find his train, then flew all the way to Middleton, NY on the first day. The only problem he encountered was keeping his trademark cigar lit in the windy *Vin Fiz*. "It's Chicago in four days, if everything goes right," he predicted, and joked that he'd better send Jimmy Ward a telegram to "watch out!"

The second day was less fortunate. Rodgers hit a tree and crashed into a chicken coop. His plane was demolished, and Rodgers was pulled from the wreckage with a bad cut on his head — but his cigar was still clamped firmly in his teeth.

The citizens of Middleton opened their Armory and pitched in to help rebuild the *Vin Fiz*. Rodgers' mechanics worked 40 hours around the clock to put the plane back together using replacement parts from the train. They knew time was pressing, because Bob Fowler, who had started from San Francisco on September 11, was already reported over the Sierra Nevada mountains.

Rodgers was soon back in the air and on his way west. Problems still continued to plague his plane. A hose broke loose, splattering Rodgers with searing hot water. When a spark plug came loose and nearly fell out, Rodgers coolly held it in place until he could land for repairs. He got lost while still traversing New York state, and when he finally landed to ask for directions, he learned he was in Scranton, Pennsylvania, 45 miles off course. Though the locals helped him get the *Vin Fiz* gassed up and in the air again, the many curiosity seekers were a nuisance. "There wasn't a mark on my plane when I started in the morning," Rodgers said later, "but in ten minutes there wasn't an inch free from pencil marks. They didn't mind climbing up to get a good spot. They liked to sit in the seat, work the levers, and finger the engine. I nearly lost my temper when a man came up with a chisel to punch his initials on one of the struts!" The same day, Rodgers learned that Jimmy Ward, who had started from New York on September 13, had dropped out of the race.

Rodgers pressed on. He crashed again over Salamanca, New York, when he piled into a barbed-wire fence. Once again his crew had to rebuild the plane, but was soon in the air and over Ohio. It was then he learned that Bob Fowler had dropped out of the race when he could not fly over the Rockies. Cal Rodgers was the only contender left.

Rodgers continued on over Ohio, where he accidentally became the first pilot to fly through a thunderstorm and live to tell about it. "The first thing I knew I was riding through an electric gridiron," he described it later. "I didn't know what lighting might to do an aeroplane, but I didn't like the idea, so I swung her and streaked it for the east." When he disappeared from view of the special train, his crew and family waited anxiously. Finally the news came that Rodgers had landed safely, about twenty miles off course.

On his best days, Rodgers could fly about 200 miles,

but accidents still plagued the trip. Taking off from Huntington, Indiana, into a headwind, Rodgers had trouble gaining altitude. He turned the *Vin Fiz* and hopped it across a field, nearly careening into the massed spectators. He was forced between two trees and under telegraph wires to avoid hitting the crowd, snagged a wing on a small rise, and crashed again.

It wasn't until October 8 that Rodgers reached Chicago. He'd flown only 1000 miles in three weeks and knew he could not reach the west coast in under thirty days. Though he could not win the Hearst prize, Rodgers was determined to continue. "I am bound for Los Angeles and the Pacific Ocean," he said. "If canvas, steel, and wire together with a little brawn, tendon, and brain stick with me, I mean to get there. I'm going to do this whether I get five thousand dollars or fifty cents or nothing. I am going to cross this continent simply to be the first to cross it in an airplane!"

Rodgers turned south, intending to cross the western mountains at their lowest point. He passed through Illinois, Missouri, and Oklahoma with few unfortunate incidents. Schools in Kansas City, Missouri were closed on the day he flew through so that the school children could watch. A newspaper in in Muskogge, Oklahoma, wrote, "To those who saw Rodgers alight and step from his machine, there came a sensation as if they had just seen a messenger from Mars."

South of Austin, Texas, a piston in the engine shattered. Rodgers was grounded again. There was a spare engine aboard the train and he was soon back in the air, only to be grounded once more near Spofford, Texas when a propeller struck the ground and splintered, causing the plane to drop so hard that the undercarriage was demolished and the wings were crumpled. The plane had to be completely rebuilt once more. Broken skids and a leaky water pump slowed the flight across Texas, but Rodgers made up for it when he crossed New Mexico in a single day. He reached Phoenix, Arizona, on November 2. The next day he reached California, but the engine exploded over the Salton Sea, driving metal shards into Rodgers' arm. He managed to land in spite of the pain. It took two hours for doctors in Imperial Junction to remove all the shards, and longer still for Rodgers' mechanics to install the old engine that had failed over Texas.

On November 5, after 49 days of flying, Rodgers reached Pasadena, California, which was the official end of the journey. There he was mobbed by a crowd of over 10,000 fans. He had covered 4,231 miles in 82 hours of actual flying time, flying an average of 51.6 miles per hour.

But Rodgers wasn't satisfied. In New York he had said he meant to wet his wheels in the Pacific, and he intended to make good on the promise. Long Beach was thirty miles away, a distance that should have been easy. A week after landing in Pasadena, Rodgers took off for Long Beach. Halfway there he lost control of his plane and crashed again, this time breaking his ankle severely. It was another month before both he and the *Vin Fiz* were ready for flight once more. On December 10, 84 days after taking off from New York, Cal Rodgers landed the *Vin Fiz* on the sands of Long Beach and rolled his plane into the surf. His plane had been rebuilt five times on the journey. The only parts that remained of the original plane were the vertical rudder and the drip pan — and, incredibly, the glass bottle of Vin Fiz syrup. To honor the achievement, the Wright Brothers paid Rodgers a royalty for every day of the flight. Roy Knaubenshue, working as the Wright representative in California, presented the prize.

"My record won't last long," he said, then made a radical prediction. "With proper landing places along the route the trip can easily be made in thirty days or less."

After partaking of the celebrations, Rodgers and his wife settled in Long Beach, California. Unfortunately, Rodgers' enjoyment of his victory was short-lived. On April 3, 1912, Rodgers took off for a flight at 3:00 in the afternoon. He turned his plane out over the ocean, then circled back and swooped low over the nearby roller coaster. He dodged a flock of seagulls, then took the plane down into a dip. Spectators on the shore saw Rodgers frantically working the levers with a surprised look on his face. He stood up as though to jump off, but was too late. The plane smashed into the breakers in two feet of water, upended, and turned over. Rodgers was pinned underneath, killed instantly when the plane dropped on him and broke his neck and back.

There were rumors that Rodgers had been drinking before the flight, but those who knew Cal Rodgers knew he never touched alcohol. Some reporters thought that reckless stunts were at fault, but Rodgers was a careful flyer who seldom took unnecessary chances. A few weeks later, Mabel Rodgers revealed the real cause of the crash: a dead seagull was wedged between the fuselage and the rudder, making it impossible to control the plane.

Rodgers was buried near his father in the Allegheny Cemetery in Pittsburgh. A large stone tablet marks the grave, adorned by a bronze reproduction of the soaring *Vin Fiz*. The real *Vin Fiz* was restored and how hangs in the National Air and Space Museum in Washington, D.C.

Chapter 7
A Woman's Place is in the Cockpit
— Harriet Quimby

Aviation in its first few years was entirely a man's world — until 1911, when a slim, dark-eyed American journalist appeared on the scene with an international pilot's license in her hand determined expression on her face. The young journalist was Harriet Quimby, a writer, drama critic, and editor for *Leslie's Illustrated Weekly* in New York.

Little is known about Quimby's early years. She was born in May of 1875 in Michigan. No one has found her birth certificate to confirm this, but census records of 1880 show her living with her parents and her older sister in Arcadia. In 1880, the farm failed and the Quimbys moved west. Few records exist that tell us where the family lived, but by 1897 Quimby and her father were listed in the city directory of San Francisco, California. Since she had her own separate listing, most biographers assume she was living on her own.

Quimby evidently tried a career in acting, as the 1900 census lists her occupation as "actress." However, at this time she was writing articles regularly for the *San Francisco Bulletin* and occasionally for other publications, which probably earned her a better salary than acting, and may have appealed more to her prodigious intellect.

New York was the place for writers, so to New York Quimby headed in 1903, followed by her parents. It took considerable courage for a young woman to live alone and support herself and her parents in New York at the time, but courage was something Quimby had in abundance. As soon as she was settled in, she began writing. She began as a contributor to *Leslie's Illustrated Weekly*, and later became a member of the staff. She wrote for other publications under various male and female pen names. Many of her articles were for women, but went far beyond mere household tips and recipes. Quimby advised women on how to find jobs, manage the household budget, live alone safely and successfully, and do household repairs. She also traveled on assignment to photograph and write about faraway places: Europe, Cuba, Mexico, and even Iceland. She interviewed actors, singers, acrobats, and comedians, a task her few years on the stage probably prepared her well for. In 1906, she covered an auto race at the Vanderbilt race track and took a high-speed ride that sparked her interest in fast machines. She soon bought her own automobile and began a series of articles advising women about auto maintenance. She also wrote eloquently about issues of her day, including voting rights for women, corrupt politics, child neglect, and the conservation of wildlife. In June of 1911 she interviewed William Hornaday, a noted wildlife conservationist, and in her article she urged her readers to write to their Senators and Representatives about the protection of birds in the United States. She wrote screenplays for the Biograph Company in New York. D.W. Griffith bought seven of her scripts, making Quimby one of the first female screenwriters.

Quimby entered the world of aviation in 1910, when she attended the Belmont Park International Aviation Tournament at Belmont Race Track in New York. Quimby was as fascinated by aircraft as she had been by fast automobiles. She met Matilde and John Moisant, brother and sister who operated the Moisant School of Aviation in Mineola along with another brother. John Moisant was one of the featured fliers of the meet, and represented the U.S. in a race around the Statue of Liberty. He had wrecked his own plane on the ground and had to buy another from a competitor, but he darted ahead of the other racers to victory. Following the race, both Quimby and Matilde enrolled in the Moisant school.

Before lessons could begin, however, John Moisant was killed in a crash at an exhibition in New Orleans. Quimby and Matilde were saddened but undeterred. Quimby continued writing for income, but turned up each morning just before dawn for flying lessons. She covered her dresses with a long duster coat and wore an aviator's leather helmet for protection. Though she was quiet about her activities, it wasn't long before the press learned that the two women were trying for a pilot's license.

Though HélPne Dutrieu and Elise de Laroche, among other women, were already flying in France to the applause of their countrymen, few American women dared to try. For one thing, there were few schools that would accept women. The Wright Brothers and Glenn Curtiss refused to even consider female students. Most men believed that women were too easily excited and temperamentally unfit to fly. Early biplanes also required a certain amount of brute force to manage, and it was believed that women simply weren't strong enough.

But Quimby, having already tried a career on stage, was unafraid of unusual pursuits. She became a sensation in the press, particularly with *Leslie's Illustrated Weekly* which helped support her efforts. Quimby took five weeks of lessons and on July 31 of 1911, she began a series of flight tests for her license. The tests were monitored by the Aero Club of New York. The tests included taking off, landing, flying figure-eights over the aerodrome, and flying at given altitudes. On August 1, Quimby set a new accuracy record for landing 7 feet, 9 inches from the mark set on the field for her. She received her *Fédération Aéronautique Internationale* certificate, becoming the first American woman to earn an international pilot's license. "Flying seems easier than voting," she remarked tartly, for women in 1911 still were not allowed to vote. Matilde Moisant passed her flight tests soon after.

On September 4 of 1911, Quimby flew over the crowd at the Richmond County Fair in a Moisant monoplane. She wore the plum-colored satin flying suit that became her trademark. Quilted for warmth, with a hood to protect her head from the winds, the suit was both stylish and practical. However, the lower half ended in bloomers instead of a skirt, shocking the sensibilities of many spectators. Quimby grew frustrated by the news articles which gave more press coverage to her wardrobe than her flying abilities. Nor was she entirely happy about reporters referring to her as New York's "Dresden China Aviatrix." She was as serious about flight as she was about writing. Quimby wrote a series of articles in which she speculated about the future of aviation. She envisioned planes large enough to carry many passengers, with scheduled stops, similar to passenger train service. She predicted worldwide air mail service, and the use of airplanes for aerial photography and mapping. She also wrote about air safety, warning potential aviators about the dangers of flying, especially the dangers of over-confidence. She advocated progress in aviation, noting that the United States was falling far behind the Europeans.

In November of 1911, Quimby and Matilde Moisant joined the Moisant International Aviators Exhibition Team for an exhibit of flying skills in Mexico City. Matilde continued flying with the team in Mexico, but Quimby returned to New York. She had another idea in mind.

Louis Blériot had flown the English Channel in 1909, but no woman had attempted the feat. Quimby decided she would be the first. Further, she would fly the route in reverse, from Dover to Calais. She kept her plans quiet for fear one of the European female flyers would try to beat her to it. She hired a manager, aeronaut A. Leo Stevens, to manage her exhibition flights and to help prepare her for the Channel flight.

In March of 1912, Quimby sailed from New York to France. Her first stop in France was the Blériot factory where she tried to buy a two-seat monoplane but none were available. Blériot himself, however, offered to lend her one, which she had shipped to Dover. Yet Blériot and even her own crew doubted she would succeed.

"I was annoyed from the start," she wrote, "by the attitude of doubt on the part of the spectators that I would never really make the flight. They knew I had never used the machine before, and probably thought I would find some excuse at the last moment to back out of the flight. This attitude made me more determined than ever to succeed."

Quimby had to wait at Dover, for the weather turned foul. It cleared on April 14, but that was a Sunday and Quimby never flew on Sundays. Disaster did not take Sunday off, however, for it was on the night of April 14, 1912 that the Titanic struck an iceberg and sank. While the sinking captured the headlines, Quimby waited two more days for good weather to return. In the meantime, pilot Gustov Hamel ferried a woman passenger across the Channel, ruining Quimby's hopes of being the first woman to cross, though she would still be the first woman to fly the Channel herself.

On the morning of April 16, the weather had cleared sufficiently that Quimby decided to try the flight. Hamel was among the crew to see her off. He gallantly offered to don her famous flying suit and impersonate her, making the flight himself while she crossed by boat, but Quimby refused. She did, however, accept his gift of a compass and his instructions on how to operate it.

"It seemed so easy that it looked like a cross-country flight," she wrote later. "I am glad I thought so and felt so, otherwise I might have had more hesitation about flying in the fog with an untried compass, in a new and untried machine, knowing that the treacherous North Sea stood ready to receive me if I drifted only five miles too far out of my course."

Knowing the Channel flight would be deathly cold, Quimby donned two layers of long underwear under her flying suit. She put on two overcoats and a sealskin stole. At the last minute, someone handed her a hot water bottle on a string, which she tied around her waist. At 5:30 in the morning, Quimby lifted off from Dover, circled around Dover castle for the movie cameras that were grinding away, and headed out over open water.

"In an instant I was beyond the cliffs and over the channel," she wrote a month later in an article titled *An American Girl's Daring Exploit*. "The thickening fog obscured my view. Calais was out of sight... There was only one thing for me to do and that was to keep my eyes fixed on the compass."

A wall of fog stood between her and the French coastline, and Quimby plowed into it. Her goggles fogged up, water dripped from all parts of the plane, and her hot water bottle soon lost its heat. With absolutely nothing to see in the thick fog, Quimby flew by guesswork alone. When she guessed she must be near land, she nosed her plane down again.

"The distance straight across from Dover to Calais is only twenty-two miles, and I knew that land must be in sight if I could only get below the fog and see it," she wrote. "So, I dropped from an altitude of about two thousand feet until I was half that height. The sunlight struck upon my face and my eyes lit upon the white and sandy shores of France."

Quimby decided not to risk tearing up the farmers' fields nearby and touched down on the hard sands instead. In moments she was mobbed by cheering fishermen and their families. They lifted her on their shoulders and carried her off for a hot breakfast. Her entire flight had lasted a little longer than 30 minutes.

Her accomplishment did not receive the press coverage it deserved back in the United States, however.

The headlines were still full of news about the Titanic disaster, and reporters had little attention for anything else.

Quimby's career came to an untimely end later in 1912. She had arranged to fly at an exhibition in Massachusetts in July. On July 1, she arrived and met William Willard, the event organizer. Willard and his son tossed a coin to see who would have the privilege of flying with Quimby, and the elder Willard won. He casually appointed Earle Ovington to succeed him if anything happened, then climbed aboard. Quimby took her monoplane up in the air on a flight over Boston Light, then circled over Dorchester Bay.

At 1500 feet, the monoplane suddenly pitched forward. Willard fell out. Quimby struggled for control, but a few seconds later she was tossed out as well. Both fell to their deaths on the mud flats below. Many reports say the plane righted itself and came to a safe landing, but the plane was in fact severely damaged as it hit the muddy water and overturned.

The cause of the accident has been debated ever since. Ovington claimed the aircraft cables tangled in the steering mechanism. The *Boston Globe* blamed the lack of seat belts, which might have, in fact, saved both pilot and passenger. Others believed that Willard, an excitable man, might have suddenly leaned forward to speak to Quimby and overbalanced the plane. The sudden loss of weight on one side would have made it almost impossible for Quimby to regain balance. When flying alone, she normally put a sandbag in the passenger seat.

Whatever the cause, that day in July of 1912, America

lost one of its most outspoken advocates for aviation progress, an independent visionary who proved that women could indeed fly.

Eddie Rickenbacker strikes a characteristically flamboyant pose, in World War I uniform.

Chapter 8
Wild Warbirds
— Eddie Rickenbacker

In 1917 the United States entered the first World War. Many U.S. pilots had already joined the British and the French armies, flying with the first military air forces in the world. One such flying ace was Eddie Rickenbacker.

Rickenbacker was born in Columbus, Ohio, in 1890. When he was twelve, his father died and Rickenbacker went to work to help support his family. Fortunately for him, Rickenbacker was an energetic worker with a driving curiosity which helped him find good jobs. In his teens he landed a job in a garage where he worked on cars and tested them. Tinkering with cars was satisfying to the mechanically-minded young man. He enrolled in a correspondence course in engineering, and about the same time applied for a job with the Frayer-Miller Automobile Company in Columbus. The owner, Lee Frayer, was impressed that the fifteen-year-old Rickenbacker was studying to be an engineer. He invited his young employee to ride with him in the 1906 Vanderbilt Cup Race. Rickenbacker was so thrilled at being in the race that he soon found his job of demonstrating cars far too tame. He preferred roaring along with the throttle wide open, and started entering car races at county fairs.

By 1910 Rickenbacker was racing full time. For the next six years he was one of the nation's leading race car drivers, racing in the Indianapolis 500 and at Daytona beach. But when war broke out in Europe, Rickenbacker's career took another turn.

Rickenbacker suggested putting together an aerial fighter squadron, thinking he would choose pilots from among his racing friends. He felt that a car racer's quick reactions and ability to make swift decisions in the middle of chaos would make them prime candidates as fighter pilots. However, quick decision-making was not a characteristic of the governmental agencies he petitioned, and Rickenbacker's request got bogged down in red tape. Instead, Rickenbacker was assigned to be driver for various officers in France. Legend has it that he was the chauffeur for General John "Black Jack" Pershing, but in his autobiography Rickenbacker stated that the story was invented by the press. He did, however, drive for the great air pioneer, William "Billy" Mitchell. Mitchell didn't appreciate his race-car-driver style of roaring through the bomb-cratered roads, however, and Rickenbacker went through a series of transfers, including a stint in the French Air Service, before he finally arrived at the 94th Aero Squadron in 1918. There his adventures as a fighter pilot in the "Hat in the Ring" Squadron began.

Warplanes at the time were fragile things, framed in wood and covered in canvas. Pilots sat in open cockpits and wore helmets, goggles, and heavy leather flying suits for protection. Some planes had machine guns which were timed so that the bullets would not strike the propeller blades, but in many cases the only artillery on board was the pistol the pilot carried. Pilots sometimes carried small bombs which they would throw out of the plane by hand.

Rickenbacker took full advantage of the

maneuverability of the little warplanes. He learned to use the sun to his advantage, keeping it behind him so that enemy pilots flew with the sun in their eyes. He also used the clouds as cover so that he could dart down and take enemies by surprise. He knew just where his adversaries' blind spots were and maneuvered into them before firing on them.

On April 29, Rickenbacker shot down his first enemy plane in a daring aerial battle over the Montsec area of France. His actions that day earned him the *Croix de Guerre* medal from the French military.

On May 17, Rickenbacker was flying a Nieuport biplane north of Saint-Mihiel in France when he noticed three German Albatros biplanes leave the ground in German-held territory and head toward the French lines. Rickenbacker followed the enemy planes at a higher altitude, and was so eager to attack the moment they crossed into French-held territory that he forgot about the dangers of German anti-aircraft guns. Two big bursts from the "Archies," as the guns were nicknamed, warned Rickenbacker that he'd been spotted. The Albatros pilots turned and saw Rickenbacker's Nieuport on their tail. Rickenbacker nosed down into a furious 200 mile-per-hour dive toward the rearmost Albatros, firing at and downing the craft as the German pilot tried to out-dive him.

The dive brought the Nieuport so close to the ground that Rickenbacker had to yank the stick back into his lap to pull the plane up into a steep climb. The force was too much for the Nieuport. The right wing collapsed. The entire upper wing canvas ripped away. The Nieuport turned over on her right side and dropped nose-down into a tailspin.

Like most pilots of his day, Rickenbacker had no parachute. His only choices were to right his airplane and attempt to land it — if possible — or ride it to his death.

Rickenbacker opened up the throttle despite the fact that he was under 3000 feet from the ground. The sudden burst of speed helped level the plane. With only the lower wing for support the Nieuport was crippled, yet Rickenbacker kept it steady. He barely noticed the exploding aerial shells from the "Archies" as he struggled to keep the plane aloft. The Nieuport could not climb, but its descent was slow enough that Rickenbacker was able to fly across the lines and into French-held territory. Though he grazed the top of the hangar as he sailed into the airfield and "pancaked" the plane down hard on the landing field, Rickenbacker walked away unhurt.

Rickenbacker's plane wasn't the only Nieuport to lose its wing canvas under strain. Rickenbacker knew he and his fellow pilots needed better planes. He went to the American Experimental Aerodrome in Orly, near Paris, where he learned to his delight that his squadron would soon receive new Spads, experimental planes which promised to be much sturdier than the flimsy Nieuports.

But the war wouldn't wait for the new planes to come in. Still flying Nieuports, Rickenbacker shot down his fifth and sixth enemy planes on May 31, earning the title of "ace." The same day he was put in command of the Hat-in-the-Ring squadron following the death of the squadron commander. Raoul Lufbery's plane, taking heavy damage from enemy fire, burst into flame. Lufbury, himself on fire, leaped to his death in an attempt to escape.

Of his squadron leader's death, Rickenbacker wrote in his diary, "We have learned to love and respect each other and then forget each other in a brief few minutes." The men of the Hat-in-the-Ring Squadron understood the dangers of flying in fragile craft, without parachutes, in the middle of a war. They accepted the dangers, and so, too, accepted death as a part of it. The morning after taking command of the squadron, Rickenbacker flew out and downed two enemy planes in one day.

By August of 1918, his entire squadron was outfitted with the new Spads which gave no more trouble with collapsing wings or torn canvas. Rickenbacker put in more combat time in enemy territory than any other pilot in his squadron. He downed twenty-two planes and four balloons. He was in the air on Armistice Day, the day the war ended, and observed soldiers on both sides below him throwing helmets in the air, firing off rockets, and jumping out of the trenches to run across the No Man's Land between the front lines and greet one another.

For his heroics during the war Rickenbacker was awarded the Medal of Honor and the Distinguished Service Cross with nine Oak Leaves from the United States, and the *Croix de Guerre* with Four Palms and the Legion of Honor Medal from France.

Following the war, Rickenbacker went into business manufacturing cars, and later founded Florida Airways, which he sold to Pan American Airways. He continued working in the commercial airline industry in management and advising positions. In 1941 he was critically injured when the airliner he was riding in crashed, but he recovered and went on to be a civilian advisor to the U.S. Army Air Service in World War II. It was during this phase of his career that Rickenbacker's strangest and most difficult adventure occurred.

In October of 1942, Rickenbacker and seven companions left Hawaii in a B-17 on an advisory mission to the South Pacific. The pilot got lost on the way to Canton Island, however, and was forced to ditch in the ocean. The passengers heaved three life rafts into the water and grabbed a few emergency rations, but most of the emergency supplies sank with the plane.

The next twenty-two days were a terrible ordeal, but Rickenbacker did everything in his power to keep the men going, resorting to bullying, sarcasm, and ridicule. One man tried committing suicide by jumping overboard, but Rickenbacker dragged him back in and accused him of cowardice. Rickenbacker later learned that the surviving men swore an oath to outlive him just for the pleasure of burying him at sea. Despite his best efforts, one of the men died of injuries suffered in the crash. His body was allowed to float away from the raft while the men recited prayers. They refused to resort to cannibalism to stay alive.

Their only water was rainwater caught wrung out of their clothing into a bucket, and the moisture from a few oranges Rickenbacker doled out. Fish caught on emergency fishing gear provided food, but it was scant and the men were starving. Once, when morale was at its lowest, a sea bird landed on Rickenbacker's hat. He grabbed it, wrung its neck, and distributed the meat among the men. The intestines he used as fish bait, keeping the men fed a little longer. After two weeks afloat, the men decided to cut one raft loose to drift off in another direction in hopes of increasing their chance of being spotted.

After three weeks, Rickenbacker's rafts were finally spotted by a search plane. The Navy had, in fact, almost given up on finding the men alive, but at the insistence of Rickenbacker's wife they made one last attempt. A Navy Catalina flying boat rescued the survivors. Rickenbacker had lost 60 pounds and was badly sunburned, but was glad to be alive, if just barely. The newspapers hailed him as "The Great Indestructible." In the meantime, the raft which set off alone drifted to an inhabited island where the men found shelter and were later rescued.

Rickenbacker continued as an advisor through the rest of World War II, then resumed his career in commercial aviation. He died of pneumonia on July 23, 1973.

Chapter 9
Queen of the Barnstormers
— Bessie Coleman

In 1920, a young African-American woman boarded a ship to cross the Atlantic. Her destination, stated on her passport application, was "England, France, and Italy." Her purpose, "to study." She studied, all right — at *École d'Aviation des Frères Caudron* at Le Crotoy in the Somme, the most famous flight school in France. On June 15, 1921, Bessie Coleman was awarded a *Fédération Aèronautique Internationale* license, becoming the first person of African ancestry in the world to be a licensed pilot.

The road she had traveled until that point had not been an easy one. Coleman was born to a sharecropper family on January 26, 1892, sixth in a string of children that would eventually number thirteen. When she was nine, her father abandoned the family and traveled to Oklahoma, sick of the the extreme discrimination and frequent lynchings in their home town of Waxahatchie, Texas. Susan Coleman, Bessie's mother, took work as a cook and maid in the home of a wealthy couple who took interest in the Colemans and made certain they had enough food and clothing. Bessie's oldest brothers left for Chicago to find work, and young Bessie was left at home to care for her younger sisters.

She resented missing out on school while waiting for the youngest of her sisters to reach school age. Further, she resented being sent out to the cotton fields with other black children to bring in the harvest. Susan Coleman, a strong believer in education, supported Bessie's desire to achieve great things. She read to the children from the Bible every night and borrowed books from a wagon library. Most of the books she chose were about well-known African-Americans and their accomplishments. Susan saw to it that her eager daughter finished eighth grade, then after letting her earn money as a laundress, enrolled her in the Colored Agricultural and Normal University. Unfortunately the money ran out before Coleman finished more than one term.

Frustrated at the hardships she faced, Coleman decided she would get nowhere struggling for a living in her little Texas town. Three of her brothers had moved to Chicago and all had work. Coleman decided to join them.

She refused to work as a cook or a laundress, work she could easily get in Texas. She saw that the beauty industry in the African-American section of Chicago was thriving, though sadly it was because of a demand for skin bleaching lotions and hair straighteners. Shrewdly, she took a job as a manicurist. Not only did she avoid the lengthy training period required for a hairdresser, but she also had a seat in the shop window where her clients enjoyed being seen having their nails done by a pretty woman. Many of her clients were wealthy and influential men, who would be of help to her later in pursuing her dreams of aviation.

Eventually her mother and sisters joined her in Chicago and also found work. When the first World War came, her older brothers John and Walter enlisted in the U.S. Army. It was a chance comment by John after the war that inspired Coleman's sudden career change.

John was teasing Coleman about the women in France, saying they were so superior to American women that they could even fly airplanes. Then he said that no black woman would ever fly. Coleman had a stubborn streak, and no sooner had brother John spoken than she decided she would be the first African-American woman to fly. In fact, she'd become the first licensed black pilot anywhere in the world.

She went in search of a flight school that would accept her but could find none. There were no black flight instructors, and no white instructor would have her. For many people that would have been the end of the dream, but Coleman was too stubborn to give up. She turned to Robert Abbot, editor of a newspaper for African-Americans, and a man who believed not only in equality of people of all colors, but also in equality of women and men.

Abbot told her that if she wanted to fly she would have to go to France. Not only was France the world's leader in aviation at the time, but discrimination against black people was far less in France than in the United States. Coleman enrolled in a language school to study French, handed her manicurist job over to her sister, and took a job managing a chili parlor to earn better wages. With her earnings and support from Abbot, who intended to report her progress in his newspaper, Coleman set off for France.

The first two schools she contacted would not take her because two women aviators had recently been killed in crashes. On her third try, at the *École d'Aviation,* Coleman was finally accepted. She took a cheap room nine miles from the airfield and walked the distance each day. She took her lessons in a French Nieuport Type 82, a 27-foot biplane with a 40-foot wingspan, delicate construction, and a tendency for the canvas to rip loose from the wings with potentially disastrous results. The plane was controlled with a stick in one hand and a rudder bar at the feet. By sitting in the front cockpit with her hands and feet on the controls, Coleman could feel what the instructor was doing even when she could not hear his shouted instructions.

After five grueling months of study, including learning how to inspect and maintain the plane, Coleman took her licensing test. To pass, she flew a 5 kilometer closed circuit course twice, climbed to an altitude of 50 meters, flew a figure eight, and landed within 50 meters of a given point, turning off the engine before touching down. This was standard practice, as the Nieuport had no brakes. On June 15, 1921, she was awarded her *Fédération Aèronautique Internationale* license. For reasons unknown, she listed her age as 25, though she was 29 at the time.

Coleman studied a two months longer in Paris before returning home in September of 1921. When she reached New York, reporters were there to greet her and snap up her story. She made the headlines of most African-American newspapers across the country, though many of the stories exaggerated her achievements. Coleman justified this, noting that for African-American aviators, the story had to be sensational to get any press coverage at all. At the same time she fought discrimination wherever she found it. Once a reporter at the Chicago

World Herald said he would do a story on her if she would pass as a white woman. Coleman laughed and promptly brought her dark-skinned mother and niece into the office. "This is my mother and this is my niece," she said. "And you want me to pass?"

Coleman soon discovered that her FAI credentials didn't amount to much in the United States, where the only way for her to make any money in aviation was through barnstorming. She returned to Europe to study stunt flying. While there she toured the Fokker plant, and had dinner with Anthony H.G. Fokker himself. Fokker outlined his plans to open a school of aviation to men and women of all colors and creeds. Coleman heartily approved of his plans, and pondered the idea of opening a school of her own for African-Americans.

When she returned to the United States, Robert Abbot gave her a job as aviation editor at his New York office, and instructed his staff to arrange an air show for her. It was rained out, and though it was rescheduled for a few days later, the crowds that showed up were disappointingly small. Coleman flew a borrowed Curtiss JN-4 "Jenny" from its maker, Glenn Curtiss. Curtiss would not let her do any stunt flying in it, but the sight of an African-American woman taking a plane in the air, flying it around a bit, and landing it again seemed to be sensational enough for the crowd.

Coleman continued flying at airshows to larger and larger crowds. She linked up with David L.Behncke, an aviation enthusiast who had been an Army Air Service instructor at the age of 19. Behncke organized Saturday airshows at the Checkerboard Airdrome outside of Chicago, booking wing-walkers, parachutists, and stunt pilots. Coleman became a regular in his shows, flying stunts and giving rides. Her nephew, Arthur Freeman, remembered seeing his Aunt Bessie fly when he was eight years old. Years later he wrote, "'My aunt's a flier!' I thought. 'And she's just beautiful wearing that long leather coat over her uniform and the leather helmet with aviator goggles! That's my aunt! A real live aviator!'"

Coleman's schedule became so hectic she had trouble meeting all the events she booked. This angered some of the powerful men who were supporting her, and suddenly she found she was facing both racism and sexism as her former supporters now began accusing her of not behaving as a woman should. Coleman sought new backers, and thought again about her plans for a flight school. Instead of risking her neck performing dangerous stunts, why not make a living as an instructor, while at the same time performing a valuable service to other African-Americans who wanted to fly?

Through her flying career, Coleman became acquainted with Robert Paul Sachs, an advertising manager for the Coast Tire and Rubber Company of Oakland, California. Sachs offered her good money if she would come and tour his factory, say something nice about it, then drop advertising literature from her plane. Coleman traveled to California and carried out the plan, then took her earnings to Los Angeles to buy a used Jenny, which she intended to be the beginning of a fleet of planes in her school. She arranged for a performance early in February of 1923 at the opening of a new fairground in Palomar Park. Unfortunately, moments after taking off the engine died and the Jenny nose-dived into the ground. Coleman was pulled from the wreckage with a broken leg, fractured ribs, cuts around her eyes and chin, and possible internal injuries. The crowd waiting to see her perform was unsympathetic and demanded a refund. Coleman, though in great pain, promised them a show as soon as she could walk again. A local reporter, disgusted by what he had witnessed, wrote scathingly about the crowd's reaction. A collection was taken up in Sachs' office, and black churches and other organizations sent funds to the local newspaper, the *Eagle*, to assist Coleman.

Coleman announced her plans to open an air school in Los Angeles. While she recuperated, she showed films of her flights in France at local church gatherings, trying to raise capital. But the money was scarce, and Coleman was forced to return to Chicago and the grueling barnstorming routine again. She performed stunts, and when a woman parachutist backed out on a performance, Coleman found a pilot to fly for her and performed the jump herself. When she found that a performance she was scheduled for was for white audiences only, she refused to perform until the sponsor backed down and allowed a mixed audience. She was troubled, however, by increasingly negative publicity due to changing managers and broken contracts. The press described her as temperamental, when in fact she was strong-willed and insistent on making her own career decisions. Her attitude was at odds with managers who were used to leading and having their clients follow.

While continuing to perform, Coleman turned to the lecture circuit, most often giving lectures to African-American women. She felt that her message was better received by women, who were also better activists. She also discovered that the white community found it easier to accept assertiveness in black women than black men.

Lectures, she soon realized, brought in more income than aerial performances. Finding hotels to stay in was a problem since few hotels allowed African-American guests, so she was often the guest of black families. She was continually struck at the fact that while African-Americans were limited in their job choices and were often forced to work for poor wages, they still found the means to build community churches, social clubs, and sports leagues, and had strong community pride.

Through her lecture circuit, Coleman became close friends of Reverend Hezakiah Keith Hill and his wife Viola, respected community activists in Orlando. Viola tried to talk Coleman into giving up barnstorming, but Coleman wasn't making enough income from lectures alone to open her school. Viola did talk her into opening a beauty shop in Orlando, and also influenced her to join their church. Coleman became so close to the Hills that she referred to them as "Mother" and "Daddy."

Through the Hills, Coleman found a new backer, Edwin M. Beeman. Beeman gave her money to make the final payment on a Jenny she was buying from an airfield in Texas. She asked that it be flown from Love Field to Orlando. It developed mechanical problems on the way, forcing the pilot, William Wils, to land several times and make repairs.

Coleman was scheduled to do a parachute jump at an airshow in Jacksonville, Florida on April 30, 1926. John Thomas Betsch, publicity chairman of the city's Negro Welfare League, was also an active aviation enthusiast who encouraged Coleman to perform. She arranged for Wils to pilot the plane.

On the morning of April 30, Coleman put on her

parachute and climbed in with Wils as her pilot. Leaving her safety belt off, since she had to be free to peer over the side, she settled in while Wils took the plane up to 2000 feet, circled for several minutes, then ascended to 3500 feet. Suddenly the Jenny's engine roared and the plane accelerated to 110 miles per hour, then went into a nosedive. At 1000 feet it went into a tailspin, then flipped over at 500 feet. Coleman fell out and hit the ground before she could get the parachute open. She was killed instantly. Wils fought to regain control of the plane, but it hit treetops and crashed into a field. Wils was pinned underneath and crushed.

Betsch appeared at the scene at the same time police arrived, while several men from the crowd tried to lift the plane off of Wils. Betsch lit a cigarette to calm his nerves and carelessly tossed the match away. It landed on fuel spilled from the plane and in minutes the Jenny was enveloped in flames. Betsch was hauled off to jail. An inspection of the charred plane later revealed that a loose wrench had gotten jammed in the control gears, probably causing the plane to go out of control. Whether it was the result of accident or sabotage, as some newspapers accused, no one ever knew.

Coleman's body lay in state at the Bethel Baptist Institutional Church in Jacksonville, where a memorial service was read over her. The Hills arranged a memorial service at their Mount Zion Missionary Baptist church in Orlando. Viola Hill accompanied the casket to Chicago, where military escort of the African American Eight Infantry Regiment of the Illinois National Guard accompanied the casket to the South Side funeral home. Coleman was buried in Section 9 of Chicago's Lincoln

Cemetery at Kedsie Avenue and 123rd St.

While her dream of an African-American flight school went unrealized in her lifetime, her many lectures inspired others to follow their dreams. Not long after her death, William J. Powell organized the Bessie Coleman Aero Groups. On Labor Day of 1931, the Aero Groups put on the first all-black air show in America. In 1932, the same groups made Coleman's dream of an African-American flying school a reality.

Chapter 10
Flying *Old Soggy*
— "Slats" Rodgers

In the early days of flight, anyone who could get any rickety crate in the air was a pilot. Floyd "Slats" Rodgers started a long career in barnstorming with a homemade plane built from Wright Brothers' plans he'd found in magazines. His career in aviation was filled with great stunts — and great trouble.

Rodgers was raised in Dark Hollow, Mississippi. When he was fifteen his family moved to Texas, and Rodgers worked on his uncle's farm for fifteen dollars a month. At the age of eighteen, he married fifteen-year-old Rosie Oliver, the daughter of a neighboring farmer. Realizing he'd need a better job to support a family, Rodgers went to Dallas and applied at a railroad office. He got on as a hostler's helper, hauling coal, sand, and water for the steam engines. In his spare moments he poked into every aspect of the railroad business, learning as much as he could since he hoped for early and fast promotions. His highest aspiration was to be a railroad engineer.

Rodgers got himself in big trouble when he tried running an engine up to the turntable himself and wrecked it, but a series of hair-raising incidents soon earned him promotions. In a near-miss accident, Rodgers fell on the tracks in front of a moving train and laid flat between the tracks as an engine passed over him. He was promoted to "call boy" immediately after, and had the responsibility of getting crew members up and on the job. When he spotted an engine moving off with no one at the controls, Rodgers jumped aboard and stopped it, earning a promotion to fireman. "Borrowing" an engine on a Sunday to take friends out to a swimming hole, then accidentally wrecking it on return earned him 29 demerits — 30 would have gotten him fired. But Rodgers earned back 25 merit points when the train running ahead of the President's Special train stalled on the tracks due to a stuck water injector. Rodgers jumped into the tank car and held his breath while he maneuvered the maze of rods and valves in total darkness, finding the stuck valve and releasing it. The lead train got underway, and President Taft's special train arrived to its destination on time. He scored another 25 merit points when a train ran over a bull on the tracks. The cowcatcher failed to turn the animal aside, and the bull's mangled carcass was caught under the coach. Rodgers went after it with an axe, getting himself soaked in gore in the process, but keeping the train on schedule.

Though Rodgers had only a few years of education, he had a keen mechanical sense. When it came time to study for the engineer's test he started sneaking engine parts into the shop he was assigned to, where he would figure out their function by blowing smoke through them. He passed his test and became an engineer.

By that time the glamor of railroading was wearing off. Rodgers had been reading about the Wright Brothers and their accomplishments in his free time. While running engines down the track, he dreamed of controlling a machine with wings.

In 1911, Rodgers cleared off space in a chicken coop

and went to work on a scale model of a Wright plane. When it was completed he mounted it on the front of his engine. Planes were so rare then that even a good scale model drew crowds of people who wanted a glimpse of it. Magazines sent photographers to get a picture, and a woman from a nearby town offered Rodgers $25 to put the plane in front of her movie house for a week.

A model plane was one thing, but what Rodgers really wanted was a plane that could fly. He gleaned all the information he could from the library and asked a draftsman to draw up plans. He and a friend started work in Rodgers' workshop at the railroad depot. Their activity drew dozens of gawkers who crowded around the shop to watch and to make dire predictions. When the crowds became a nuisance, Rodgers' father helped him rent a house outside of town, and the men moved their workshop there.

When the plane was finished Rodgers hauled it out of doors, put a tent up over it, and charged curiosity-seekers fifty cents to see it. He made $700 in three days. The almost universal opinion of the spectators was that Rogers would never get the craft to fly — or, if he did manage to get it into the air, he would certainly kill himself.

But Rodgers was determined to fly the thing. There were no airfields and no instructors nearby so he had teach himself. The best thing he could do, he figured, was to roll the plane around on the ground a while and work the controls until he understood them completely. "Grasscutting," as this was known, was a common teaching technique.

He found it wasn't as easy as he thought. The plane waggled back and forth across the field as Rogers struggled with controls. The crowd howled with laughter, and Rodgers thought to himself, "I'll dive at you someday and freeze those giggles."

He spent six weeks "grasscutting" in his spare time. One day as he was rolling down the field he spotted a ditch directly in front of him. With no brakes on the craft, his only choices were to bail out or to take off. He jumped the plane over the ditch and sailed another 200 yards. It pancaked down in the field, smashing the landing gear. The crowd gathered to look sadly at the wreckage. Someone passed a hat around to collect money to repair the damages.

Rodgers pieced the machine back together and had it in the air again, but controlling it was still a problem. The right wing tended to sag, and because of the "soggy" wing, Rodgers dubbed his plane *Old Soggy No. 1*.

Rodgers' first paid flight happened in 1913, when a local politician paid him $400 to fly over the courthouse while the politician gave a speech. He'd never flown over 100 feet in the air before, but he was game to try. He rolled *Old Soggy* down the field, up onto a knoll, and bounced the machine into the air. The ship sailed over the courthouse on schedule, and Rodgers set it down in a peanut field.

His second paid flight, however, was the end of *Old Soggy*. The Woodmen of the World, a men's civic club, asked Rodgers to fly the plane over their picnic. Rodgers took off on schedule, but the "soggy" wing dipped and caught the ground, nosediving the machine into the field. Rodgers was trapped inside with boiling water from the radiator pouring down on his back as he struggled to unfasten the safety belt. Badly scalded, he finally got loose and crawled out. He had the plane repaired, but no one offered him any more contracts. Professional flyers from the Wright and Curtiss schools were touring the country in their sleek machines, and people lost interest in Rodgers' homemade plane. He hauled *Old Soggy* behind a barn and left it to rot.

It wasn't until 1916 that Rodgers took up flying again as a civilian instructor to the U.S. Army Air Service. He trained pilots until the pilots themselves were skillful enough to be instructors, which put Rodgers out of a job. He went back to driving engines again. On one train run, Rodgers was approached by a man in Oklahoma who offered to pay him $30 for a case of whiskey, which Rodgers could buy for $10 a case in Texas. Oklahoma was a "dry" state — laws there forbade the selling of liquor. His wife protested when she learned about it, but the lure of easy money was too great. Later when Prohibition began nationwide, Rodgers went into full-time bootlegging. Over the years he would lose his wife, his family, and his health to smuggling and bootlegging, but at the time Rodgers wanted fast cash. With money from bootlegging and from shrewd investments in wildcat oil wells, Rodgers bought a Lincoln Standard airplane and took up barnstorming to provide a cover occupation to his illegal business.

Hardened by his new associates, and troubled after his wife left him, Rodgers grew into a reckless flyer who would do just about anything in the air if there were a paycheck at the other end of it. He knew that audiences gathered at airshows not just to see pilots fly stunts, but also for the morbid thrill of watching them crash and die. For one show, he teamed up with Gene Brewer, a well-known wing-walker, and rigged up a sawdust-stuffed dummy which he meant to shove out of the plane to make it look as though Brewer had fallen. They flew a 3:00 show with Brewer's usual daring stunts on the wings of the plane. For the 5:00 show, Rodgers shoved the dummy into the cockpit and climbed in with it. He took the plane up to 1500 feet and began a loop. At the top of the loop he let go of the dummy. It twisted and whirled to the ground. An ambulance team that was in on the plan raced to the scene ahead of all the others, stuffed the dummy into the ambulance, and went roaring off to the hospital with sirens blaring. The police cleared the way. When they arrived at the hospital, the police were furious when they saw they'd been escorting not an injured performer, but a battered dummy. They hauled Rodgers off to jail, charging him with endangering the lives of others who might try his same tricks. The mayor, however, intervened. He'd been to the airshow and thought the trick was thrilling. "You all don't have anything on these fellows," the mayor said. "They were outside the city limits."

Just before one show, in which Rodgers was to fly stunts in a refurbished Curtiss Jenny, he was approached by an elderly music professor who wanted a ride in the plane to Witchita. Rodgers told him to be ready in a half an hour, as he was giving the plane a pre-flight inspection. Before the man returned, Major Bill Long, a friend of Rodgers in the airplane business, came along with something interesting.

"Slats, I've got something to help out with the show."

"Let's have it," Rodgers said.

"I've got a wind-driven siren. Let's put it on your landing gear and give them some noise up there."

Rodgers shrugged. "Put on a monkey and a hand organ if you want to."

Long fastened on the siren and rigged up a switch to inside the cockpit so Rodgers could control it from there. As Long worked, Rodgers finished his inspection and saw that the throttle switch he'd asked the mechanics to repair hadn't been fixed properly. He wanted tubing for the throttle rod instead of the usual piano wire because the wire kept breaking. The throttle had not only been repaired with wire, but it had been welded in place. There was no time to fix it since his passenger had already returned. Hoping the repair would hold, Rodgers helped the professor into the plane and climbed into the cockpit.

A mechanic gave the propeller a turn and the engine started right up, startling both the mechanic and the pilot. The mechanic could have been killed by the turning propeller. Rodgers tried to cut the ignition but the switch would not work. The mechanic shouted that he, too, was flying to Witchita, and would meet Rodgers there to repair the plane.

Rodgers took off in spite of the broken ignition switch. Well into the flight he decided to test the siren. The switch in the cockpit worked fine and the siren screamed as expected. He flipped the switch to turn it off — and the siren kept on screaming. The switch had broken.

Rodgers swore, as the noise of the siren above the roar of the plane was deafening. He hoped his passenger was doing all right. The professor grinned back at him, seeming to enjoy the music of the siren.

Rodgers noticed that the engine was running fast and tried to pull back on the throttle, but nothing happened.

The welded wire had snapped. Now he was truly in a fix. His only option was to fly the plane until it ran out of gas, then attempt a dead-stick landing. The Jenny had a Hispano-Suiza motor, one of the best available to barnstormers, but Rodgers wondered if it could hold together under the strain.

Hold it did, for another hour and fifteen minutes as Rodgers circled the airfield at Witchita. When the Jenny finally ran out of gas, Rodgers nosed her down. Just as she was setting down on the landing strip, gas ran from the lines into the carburetor and the engine roared to life again. Rodgers took her back into the air and made a tight turn, knowing the gas would not last long. It ran out halfway through the turn. He took the plane down again and jumped out as soon as she hit the ground. He grabbed the left wing. The engine started again, and Rodgers dug in with his heels, keeping the plane turning in a small circle, with the siren still screaming, until the gas ran out. The whole time he kept yelling at his passenger to stay in, because the man kept trying to climb out.

When he finally came to a halt and helped his passenger out, the men from the airfield came running out from under cover and asked what was the matter.

"You think of something that ain't the matter," Rodgers growled.

One summer Rodgers was asked to do a night show at Love Field. A show promoter wanted someone to fly a plane covered with fireworks, and Rodgers was the only pilot anyone knew who was crazy enough to try it. He agreed, and the ship was wired so that all he had to do was push a button to start the show.

On the first run, Rodgers took the plane up to 3,000

feet, then pushed the button. The fireworks all lit up as planned, but the sparks and smoke were in Rodgers' face and he could not see. Holding the plane level was almost impossible, and Rodgers went into a spin to the right. No sooner had he recovered than he spun to the left. He was losing altitude fast when the fireworks finally fizzled out. Once his vision recovered, he could spot the lights of Dallas and soon found Love Field again. The crowd was whooping and cheering when he landed, honking auto horns and yelling.

"Finest acrobatics we've ever seen!" one man said.

"Acrobatics, hell!" Rodgers snarled back. "I was fighting for my life."

The man only laughed.

Rodgers repeated the trick one more time, but this time he had a long tube made of tin that would reach from the rear cockpit up close to the engine. When the fireworks blazed up, Rodgers had a clear view through the tin tube. He lined himself up with the lights of Dallas and held the plane level until all the fireworks went out. It was a far easier flight, but the crowd didn't like it as much.

When parachutes were first coming out, not many people wanted to use them. In 1922, an agent for a parachute company offered Rodgers $1,500 to demonstrate the company's parachute. That much honest money was tempting, but Rodgers suspected that the large price meant a job no one else would want. "All you have to do," the man explained, "is take up an old Jenny and set it afire. Then you bail out of it and come drifting down in a parachute."

Rodgers took the job. An electrician wired the ship so Rodgers could just push a button to set it on fire. The electrician stuffed the wings and front cockpit with oil-soaked rags, then wired it up to large batteries. Wire ends in the oiled rags were set to glow red-hot when the button was pushed, setting the rags aflame.

A crowd of over 15,000 jammed the field, and crowd control was so poor that the audience was soon overrunning the space in the middle of the field where the plane was supposed to fall. Rodgers tried flying low over the crowd to disperse them but they still jammed right in. He knew he couldn't just abandon the stunt, because an angry mob was more danger to him than a crashed plane. Crowds had been known to attack and nearly kill pilots when their planes wouldn't work and they could not perform as promised.

Rodgers took the plane up and figured the people below would just have to look out for themselves. At 2000 feet he undid his safety belt and touched the button. Nothing happened. Rodgers circled away from the field long enough to rummage around the cockpit for some matches. He dragged some of the oily rags from the front cockpit and after two tries got them burning. He threw the flaming rags into the front cockpit where they blazed up, and Rodgers jumped.

The ship passed him up in a spin as he floated down. The whole plane was alight, with fire and smoke streaming out, to the thrill of the audience. The ship crashed so close to some cars with people sitting in them that it threw mud all over the cars.

After many years of barnstorming and smuggling, Rodgers finally decided to go straight when he was nearly killed by a jealous girlfriend who hit him in the head with an axe. He had already outlived most of his contemporaries and had lived through more adventures and close scrapes than most pilots could brag about. Of the "easy" money he'd gotten from smuggling he had nothing left. Most of it had either been spent or had been confiscated by the police. Rodgers took up crop dusting and barnstorming to earn a living.

On his crop dusting routes he discovered a house where a young divorced woman lived with her parents and her children. The children would come out and wave at him as he flew by. He bought an evening paper, wrapped a package of candy in it, and dropped it in her yard on his way home. He repeated this for several weeks running before he touched down nearby and met the woman. After a brief courtship they married and moved to a ranch. The ranch business didn't pan out as Rodgers wasn't much of a rancher. He sold it an opened a steak house, later selling that and opening a camp ground for hunters and anglers on the Rio Grande. There he and his new wife remained until they retired.

Chapter 11
From Airmail to the Atlantic
— Charles Lindbergh

Neither rain nor snow nor sleet nor heat nor gloom of night stays these couriers from the swift completion of their appointed rounds," reads the inscription on the New York City post office building. While never the official motto of the Post Office Department as many believe, the inscription certainly describes the determined attitude of the early mail pilots.

Charles Lindbergh is best known for making the first solo crossing of the Atlantic by air 1927. Lieutenant Commander Albert Read and his crew made the first crossing in 1919 in a Navy-Curtiss flying boat, flying from Newfoundland to the Azores, then to Portugal. Two weeks later, John Alcock and Arthur Brown made the first non-stop Atlantic flight, flying their converted Vickers Vimy bomber from Newfoundland to Ireland in 16 hours and 20 minutes. Over ninety other crews had flown across the Atlantic since then, but no one had made a solo flight. And no one had attempted the long New York to Paris route that Lindbergh flew.

But before the Atlantic adventure, Lindbergh was racking up flight hours as a mail pilot. Airmail was expensive and something of a novelty at the time. Many daring young pilots flew the mail routes, first in aging "Jennies" left over from the first World War, and later in DH-4s, which the pilots nicknamed "flying coffins." The

Charles Lindbergh in front of his plane, The Spirit of St. Louis, on May 20, 1927 as he prepared for his historic solo flight from New York to Paris.

name was apt. The engines had a tendency to overheat until they glowed, and the undercarriage often collapsed during a crash landing, pinning the pilot between the engine and the mail load. Night flights were responsible for many crashes, since the planes flew with the most primitive of instruments — or none at all. Of the first forty pilots hired by the Postal Office Department in 1918, thirty-one had died in crashes by 1925.

This didn't deter the boldest of mail pilots, who encountered adventures that recalled the days of the Pony Express. Pilots endured emergency landings, made special deliveries, and one pilot saved a family from a house fire when he spotted the blaze from the air and flew low over the house, awakening the family in time to escape.

Lindbergh himself had a bizarre adventure when he was flying at night and encountered a thick fog over Illinois on his way to Maywood, which was Chicago's air mail port. Unable to see a safe landing place, he circled above the fog, trying to drop a flare to light his way. He could see the lights of towers, but he could not see the barrels of gasoline that the field crew was burning to attract his attention.

Lindbergh kept track of the amount of fuel he had by time rather than gallons. Thinking that his 110 gallon main tank had been filled when he set out, he calculated the time he had left and continued flying. Suddenly the engine cut out far earlier than he expected. He switched to the reserve tank, and when the engine did not pick up as soon as he expected, he reached for his flashlight and prepared to jump. Just then the engine started up again. Lindbergh figured he had about twenty minutes of flying time left.

He spotted another light and tried lowering a flare, but could see only fog. When the engine finally died, Lindbergh stepped up on the cowling and jumped, pulling the rip cord after falling about 100 feet. He aimed his flashlight down through the fog, trying to see the ground before he hit it, when to his great surprise he heard his plane's engine start up again. When he'd jumped the engine was dead, so he'd neglected to flip the engine's shutoff switch. The small amount of fuel left in the line drained into the carburetor when the plane nosed down, causing the engine to start up on its own.

Lindbergh shoved his flashlight into a pocket and pulled on the ropes of the parachute, trying to slip it out of the way before the spinning propeller cut into the parachute or its lines — or himself. The runaway plane spiraled around him, falling at about the same rate as he was. At last it dropped into the foggy darkness and disappeared.

Lindbergh reached for his flashlight, but it was missing, having fallen from his pocket in his maneuvers. Blindly he descended until he could just make out the outlines of a corn field in time to prepare before he hit the ground. He hurriedly packed up the parachute and hiked to the nearest farmhouse, where he was able to call for help. A few moments later he got a call saying that the plane was found, wrecked, in a field two miles from where he had touched down. It had narrowly missed a farmhouse before it crashed in a cornfield. The mail pit was broken open and one bag of mail was spilled on the ground, but the remaining mailbags were intact and the spilled mail was uninjured.

Lindbergh later learned that the 110 gallon tank had been removed for repairs and replaced with an 85 gallon tank. Without a proper fuel gauge, he had no way of knowing how soon he would run out of fuel.

In 1919, hotel operator Raymond Orteig had offered a prize of $25,000 to the first person who flew an airplane solo across the Atlantic, flying non-stop from New York to Paris. Lindbergh had heard about the prize, and knew that no one had succeeded in meeting Orteig's challenge. In 1927, he decided he would try for it.

Lindbergh was not the only one trying for the prize. Among the pilots who were preparing to take on Orteig's challenge was Admiral Richard E. Byrd, a famous explorer. Byrd had already made his claim to aviation fame by flying a three-engine Fokker EVIII-3m, the *Josephine Ford*, over the north pole in 1926. Newspapers and the public at large believed that out of all the contenders, Byrd had the best chance.

Lindbergh believed that his years as a mail pilot, flying in all sorts of weather day and night, gave him as much

The huge and excited crowd at Les Bourget Airfield, Paris, just after the historic flight.

experience in the air as Byrd. All he needed was an airplane that could fly the distance. Lindbergh went to the Ryan Aircraft factory in southern California. There he ordered a modified Ryan Brougham cabin plane with a 46 foot wingspan and the pilot at the rear so that extra gas tanks could be added under the wings. Among the men working on the plane was a young pilot named Douglas Corrigan who would make headlines with an unauthorized Atlantic crossing of his own eleven years later.

The men at the factory knew that other pilots were preparing to compete for the Orteig prize, and they assembled the plane as fast as they could. Not only was their pride on the line; they were also afraid that the other pilots might make the flight and take the Ortieg prize before they could get their plane out of the factory doors, which would have meant a canceled order and no more work.

On April 28, 1927, the plane was completed. Lindbergh took it up for a test flight the same day. Because the front pilot's seat had been replaced by gas tanks and the windshield covered over, Lindbergh could not see out the front. He had to peer through a periscope to see forward, and navigated mostly by compass and by what he could see out of the side windows. He named his plane the *Spirit of St. Louis*, which came as something as a surprise to the workers at the California-based company. For the next two weeks he put the plane through its paces in flight after flight, and had the factory mechanics fix any problems he found. When all was satisfactory, Lindbergh flew the plane non-stop to St. Louis, stopped overnight, then flew non-stop to New York.

When Lindbergh arrived in New York, several other

pilots were already there, waiting for the weather to clear for take-off. Among them was Admiral Byrd. Four pilots had already tried taking off despite the weather, and all four attempts ended in crashes. Two of the crashes had been fatal, and the remaining pilots were reluctant to take any chances.

Just before dawn on the morning of May 20, 1927, Lindbergh decided he had waited long enough. The weather looked better, and if he didn't get started, Byrd would surely take off before him. While ground crews filled the tanks with 451 gallons of fuel, Lindbergh stocked the cockpit with sandwiches, coffee, and two canteens of water. He had never flown the plane with the tanks completely full. The plane was so heavy with fuel that it moved sluggishly across the field. After several tries, Lindbergh finally got it into the air, barely clearing the telephone lines at the end of the runway. It was 7:52 in the morning, and Lindbergh was on his way to Paris.

He had already planned his route. Rather than following a straight line drawn on a flat map, Lindbergh followed what is called the Great Circle Route. Because of the curvature of the earth, his flight path would be shorter if he headed slightly northward toward Boston, Nova Scotia, and Newfoundland. He headed over the Atlantic from Newfoundland, still angling northeast. When he was nearly halfway across, the circle route would take him southwest, and on to France.

And he would have to make it with the fuel he had, with no chance to refill his tanks. To conserve fuel, Lindbergh flew close to the water where the air tended to be smoother. Only when he encountered a storm did he fly higher, rising to 10,000 feet so that he could fly above the storm. In one of his autobiographies, *We*, Lindbergh described conditions as he neared the storm:

> As I approach those storm clouds, air is really getting rough. Wing tips flex with rapid, jerking movements, and the cockpit bumps up, down, and sideways.
>
> The wings were never designed for such a wrenching! I feel as though the storm were gathering my plane in its teeth as a dog picks up a rabbit. If only I had a parachute! But there's no use wishing for things I don't have.

By the afternoon, Lindbergh was feeling the effects of fatigue and was wishing he could lie down and rest. To stay awake, he pulled the plane up several hundred feet above the sea and stretched and wriggled as much as he could while holding onto the controls. He knew night was coming, and worried about how he was going to stay awake.

When night fell, Lindbergh navigated by the stars and by his compass as much as he could. He had ordered the plane to be built without special night-flying instruments in order to save weight. The *Spirit of St. Louis* was too unstable to fly on instruments alone, anyway. The slightest relaxation of pressure on the rudder could send it off course.

Later than night, Lindbergh flew into a towering cloud that obscured the stars and was forced to rely only on his basic flight instruments — a compass, an altimeter, a bank-and-turn indicator, and an airspeed indicator. Flying blind, difficult enough in smooth air, required intense concentration in the swirling, stormy air inside the night-darkened cloud. Lindbergh rose to find more stable air, but flew straight into a greater problem:

> It's cold up here — I glance at the altimeter — 10,500 feet — *cold* — good Lord, there *are* things to be considered outside the cockpit! How could I forget! I jerk off a leather mitten and thrust my arm out the window. My palm is covered with stinging pinpricks. I pull the flashlight from my pocket and throw its beam onto a strut. The entering edge is irregular and shiny — ice!

Uncertain whether he could turn back, Lindbergh flew on through canyons of clouds until he could safely reach a lower elevation where the ice melted.

The very instability of the plane kept Lindbergh awake — and alive — during the flight. The *Spirit of St. Louis* required constant attention and Lindbergh was forced to stay awake to keep her level and on course. Even so, while flying through a seemingly endless fog, he was haunted by strange hallucinations as his over-fatigued brain tried to dream in spite of his being awake.

At long last he saw sunlight piercing the fog. He rose and found a patch of blue sky, and realized he'd veered north while he'd been daydreaming. But the bright sunlight helped wake him up and keep him alert. When he spotted a fishing boat out on the water he rejoiced, as he knew he must be near land.

It wasn't until mid-afternoon that he spotted what looked like a strip of low-lying fog on the northeast horizon. He realized it wasn't fog at all, but the coast of Ireland. Quickly he checked his charts and found his location, near Valentia and Dingle Bay on Ireland's southwest coast. He was almost exactly on route. A few hours later he flew across England, and soon crossed the English Channel with far less thought and in far less time than Louis Blériot's flight just eighteen years earlier. By the time he reached the coast of France, Lindbergh had set a new world distance record for nonstop airplane flight.

Night fell, and Lindbergh spotted Paris by its glow on the horizon. He saw a column of lights that could only be the Eiffel Tower. He headed toward it and circled once above it, then looked for a landing field. He soon found the field at Les Bourget, northeast of Paris. He was wide awake, but so numb from the long flight that he felt as uncoordinated as a student pilot on a first flight. Carefully he eased his craft down on the field at 10:00 in the evening, May 21. He had hardly come to a stop when the field was covered with people running toward him. In moments the plane was covered with excited spectators, who badly tore the fabric of the fuselage in their frantic efforts to take home bits as souvenirs. His total flight time had been 33 hours and 30 minutes, breaking all long-distance records at the time and winning him the Orteig prize.

Chapter 12
"For the Fun of It"
— Amelia Earhart

Of all the women in the field of aviation, Amelia Earhart is the most famous, and deservedly so. Though she is best remembered for her long-distance flights, her contributions to the scientific progress of aviation were immense.

Earhart was born in Atchison, Kansas in 1897. As a child, she enjoyed sports and outdoor play. Encouraged by her book-loving family, Earhart developed a love of reading and study. It was a good thing she enjoyed travel as well, because her father was a railroad man and the family moved frequently. Despite attending six different high schools, Earhart graduated on time.

When she visited a sister in Toronto in 1917, Earhart saw many men who had been wounded in the first World War. Earhart decided to train as a nurse's aide, thinking she would enjoy a career where she could help suffering people. Because she had studied chemistry in high school, she got a job in a hospital dispensary, where she made up prescriptions. While working in Toronto, Earhart first became interested in flying. She tried a few flying lessons in 1918.

After the war ended, Earhart studied medicine at Columbia University, but soon realized that being a doctor was not for her. She moved to California, intending to work on a degree in medical research, but decided to get a pilot's license. She worked as a telephone operator to pay for the lessons. A year later she passed all the coursework and took her solo flight. After earning her license, Earhart performed in flying shows and exhibitions. In 1922 she set a new women's altitude record of 14,000 feet.

Earhart returned to Columbia University, where she took science classes that interested her but did not pursue a degree. In 1924 she moved to Boston to visit a sister and to find work. After trying several jobs, she took a position at a settlement house called Denison House. This was a charitable organization which helped poor immigrants get settled in their new country. Earhart taught English to Syrian and Chinese immigrants and helped run youth recreation programs. Despite her busy schedule, Earhart continued flying when she could. She started plans with fellow pilot Ruth Nichols to form an organization for women pilots.

In the middle of a busy day at the settlement house, Earhart got a phone call from from a Captain H.H. Railey, who asked if she would be willing to do something for aviation which might be hazardous, though he would not reveal what. Curious, Earhart agreed to meet him that evening.

Railey told her about Mrs. Frederick Guest who was organizing a trans-Atlantic flight. Guest intended to ride as a passenger and become the first woman to fly across the Atlantic. She had already purchased a tri-motor Fokker from Admiral Byrd, which she named the *Friendship,* and had hired a pilot and mechanic. But Guest was having second thoughts about being a passenger. She asked Railey to find a young woman who was interested in aviation to make the trip. Earhart readily agreed to the flight. She knew at the start that she would receive no money for the trip, even though pilot Wilmer Stultz was to be paid $20,000 and his mechanic, Lou Gordon, would get $5,000. Her only condition was that she be allowed to fly the plane for part of the trip.

Neither Earhart nor those involved wanted a lot of advance publicity, just in case something went wrong. Earhart did not even tell her parents or her co-workers, though she wrote "popping off" letters ahead of time — farewell letters in case she did not survive the trip. "Hooray for the last grand adventure!" she put in a letter to her father. "I have no faith we'll meet anywhere again, but I wish we might."

The *Friendship* took off from Trepassy Bay in Newfoundland on June 17, 1928. The destination was Ireland. The plane almost immediately flew into fog and clouds, which disappointed Earhart. She did not have enough instrument training to fly on instruments alone. Stultz stayed at the controls during most of the flight, and Earhart spent her time keeping a log of the flight and checking their progress. She later used her notes to write a book titled *20 hours, 40 minutes*, the story the flight of the *Friendship*.

At several points they were able to fly above the clouds. Stultz took the plane as high as 11,000 feet, trying to stay above the cloud cover, but as dawn broke again the clouds piled too high to fly above without wasting fuel. They were flying by dead reckoning; their radio had ceased working about 8:00 on the first evening out.

Figuring they must be near Ireland, the crew decided to descend. As they came out of the fog, they did not spot land, but did see a large transatlantic ship crossing their path from north to south. This worried them, as they thought ships of that size should be sailing east-west. Earhart wrote out a request that the captain paint bearings on the deck for the pilots to read. She put the note in a bag, weighted it with a couple of oranges, and dropped it. Unfortunately she missed the ship. Unwilling to waste more fuel in circling, Stultz decided to move on.

As it turned out later, the ship was the *America*, sailing south from Ireland down the Irish Sea. The captain usually had bearings painted on the deck every two hours when he heard a transatlantic flight was underway, just in case any passed over his ship. But since none ever had, he had given up on the idea and had no paint ready.

So the flyers sailed on, unaware that they were passing just a few miles south of Ireland. They continued east, hoping to make land soon. Thirty minutes after passing the ocean liner, they spotted several fishing vessels, a sign that land could not be too far off. At last they spotted a coastline. Stultz dropped the *Friendship* into the first safe harbor because it was fitted with pontoons, and the fuel was too low to risk crossing the land. With only a few gallons left, Stultz taxied to a marking buoy where the crew tied the plane. The crew sat down to wait for someone to come out and welcome them.

The villagers, however, had no idea the *Friendship* was on her way, and probably thought she was a seaplane from somewhere nearby. Time passed, and finally a few people gathered on the shoreline. Gordon called to them, asking for a boat, but no one responded. Earhart waved a white towel as a sign of distress. A man on the shore took off his coat and waved back. Some time later some boats came out, and the flyers explained their situation. They learned they had landed at Burry Port, Wales, having overshot their target.

After the villagers helped them refuel, Earhart did some of the flying on the stretch from Burry Port to Southampton the next day, the only flying she got to do during the trip. Stultz landed the plane in a crowded harbor at Southampton, where enthusiastic souvenir hunters made off with most of the charts and paraphernalia of the flight.

Earhart was astonished at the amount of press she received for being a passenger on the flight. She felt she had done nothing, since she hadn't flown the plane over the ocean. She was more pleased by her visit to Lady Astor during her two weeks in London when the gracious lady took her aside and said, "I'm not interested in you a bit because you crossed the Atlantic by air. I want to hear about your settlement work."

On her return, Earhart took a small plane she had bought in England and flew across the U.S. and back, just for some recreation and to get away from the press. It turned out to be the first solo journey from the Atlantic to Pacific coast and back again made by a woman. Without realizing it, she had set another record.

Earhart took a position with *Cosmopolitan* magazine as Aviation Editor. She answered questions about aviation, and encouraged parents to let their children, boys and girls alike, learn to fly if they wanted to.

Soon after, Earhart took a position with a passenger line, Transcontinental Air Transport. Her job was to make flying appealing to women, as it was thought at the time that women were more afraid of flying than men. Earhart soon found this was not true. In 1929, Earhart entered the first women's transcontinental air race, which humorist Will Rogers called the "Powder-Puff Derby." In *For the Fun of It*, one of her autobiographical books, Earhart wrote,

> Will Rogers was on the loud speaker to point out the humorous aspects of such an event. Taking their cue from him, newspaper men coined descriptive names for the affair before contestants reached their first stop. It was generally called the 'powder puff derby' and those who flew in it variously as "Ladybirds," "Angels," or "Sweethearts of the Air." (We are still trying to get ourselves called just "pilots.")

The race started in Santa Monica, CA, on August 18, and ended at Cleveland, OH on August 26. To be eligible for the race, contestants had to have a current license and 100 hours of solo flying time. Twenty women turned out for the race, including Hollywood stunt flyer Florence "Pancho" Barnes, skydiver and instructor Phoebe Omlie, long-distance flier Ruth Nichols, and endurance flyers Bobbi Trout and Louise Thaden. The race covered 2,800 miles at about 300 miles per day. Navigation was by dead reckoning, helped with magnetic compasses and ordinary road maps. Pilots flew from sunup to sundown, rising at 4:00 to be in the air by 6:00, maintaining their machines in the evening, enduring autograph hounds and curiosity seekers every time they refueled. Fifteen pilots finished the race. Bobbi Trout cartwheeled during an emergency landing in California, coming out without a scratch though her plane was badly damage. Pancho Barnes clipped a parked car and cracked up, walking away from the wreckage. Margaret Perry flew for two days with a temperature before giving up in Fort Worth, TX, where she was hospitalized with typhoid fever. The only casualty was Marvel Crosson, who bailed out of her plane at too low an altitude and was killed when she hit the ground, wrapped in the folds of her partially unopened parachute.

While Earhart did not win the race, she recognized the bonds that had formed between the women who competed in it. She revived her plans with Ruth Nichols to form an organization of women pilots. On November 2, 1929, she and Nichols met with twenty-four other women at Curtiss Field in Valley Stream, Long Island, to form the Ninety-Nines, named for the number of charter members. The organization is still going strong today.

In 1931, after seven proposals and much consideration, Earhart married her publicist, George Putnam. They'd been friends ever since the *Friendship* flight, and though Earhart was wary of marriage for herself, the partnership seemed to work.

Ever since she flew in the *Friendship*, Earhart had wanted to fly the Atlantic herself. Soon after their marriage, Putnam arranged for Earhart to appear in ads for many different products, including a line of women's clothing. Through this "zoo part" of her career, as Earhart put it, she was able to raise funds for serious flying. With the ample cash, she bought a Lockheed Vega and had it reconditioned for the flight. "It was clear in my mind that

I was undertaking the flight merely for the fun of it," Earhart wrote. "It was, in a measure, a self-justification — a proving to me, and to anyone else interested, that a woman with adequate experience could to it."

On May 19, 1932, she took off from Grace Harbor, Newfoundland, shortly after noon. Her intended destination was Paris, France. For the first few hours she flew at 12,000 feet in an easy flight. Then the altimeter failed and remained broken the rest of the flight. Four hours out, she saw that flames were coming through a broken weld on the exhaust manifold ring. She knew it would grow worse but hoped the manifold would last until she reached land.

At 11:30 that night she flew into a severe electrical storm, but she kept her course. She tried to drop below the clouds and the Vega went into a spin. The barograph later revealed a sudden drop of 3000 feet at one point during the spin. She righted the plane at last, with whitecaps visible below. The storm lasted for at least an hour before Earhart was clear of it. As the weather calmed, she tried climbing out of the clouds for clearer skies, but noticed the plane was icing up. The tachometer froze and failed. She dropped down to get the ice to melt, dropping until she could see waves on the ocean below. Then a fog came in, and she was forced to find a middle level — high enough to use instruments safely, low enough that the plane would not ice up. Without an altimeter this was tricky. A directional gyro she'd had installed before the trip was a lifesaver, keeping her on course though flying completely blind.

At daylight she was flying between two layers of clouds, and could see the ocean through breaks in the

lower layer. She rose in altitude, though ice formed on the leading edges of the wings.
The last two hours were the hardest. The exhaust manifold was vibrating badly. When she turned on the reserve tanks she saw that the gauge was leaking. Realizing she could not safely reach Paris, she changed her course slightly to head due east to Ireland, meaning to land as soon as she could. She was afraid she'd drifted southward in the storm, but soon found that she had hit Ireland right in the middle — she was right on course. She found a cow pasture to land in. An astonished farmer said she was near Londonderry. The flight had lasted 15 hours, 18 minutes, the fastest crossing on record. "Some features of the flight I fear have been exaggerated," she later wrote. "It made a much better story to say I landed with but one gallon of gasoline left. As a matter of fact, I had more than a hundred. I did not kill a cow in landing — unless one died of fright."

After her solo Atlantic flight, Earhart made several transcontinental flights, setting new distance and speed records. The press began to wonder if she had bigger goals in mind, and indeed she did.

Late in December of 1934, Earhart and Putnam sailed to Honolulu with the Vega lashed to the deck of the S.S. *Lurline*. Reporters on board discovered that Earhart was going for a $10,000 prize offered by Hawaiian businessmen for the first person to fly from Hawaii to California. Unfortunately, rivals of the Hawaiian businessmen accused the group of using Earhart's fame to manipulate sugar tariffs. The alarmed businessmen asked Earhart to give up the flight. Stunned, she accused the men of cowardice. "I intend to fly to California within this next week with or without your support," she told them. As she left the room, the men reconsidered and decided to support her flight after all.

On January 11, 1935, Earhart was ready for takeoff, but the weather turned again and dumped rain on Honolulu. At 4:30 there was a break in the storm, and she decided it was now or never. The field was inches deep in mud, and as Earhart looked out the cockpit window, she noticed three fire engines and an ambulance following her, along with a detachment of soldiers all carrying fire extinguishers.

Grinning at their obvious pessimism, Earhart opened the throttle and released the brakes. The Vega slogged down the runway. Ahead was a pair of checkered flags that marked the point at which she would either have to lift off or hit the brakes. Paul Mantz, her mechanic, dashed alongside shouting, "Get that tail up — get that tail up!" Moments later she was airborne. She took the plane up to 5000 feet and soared over Diamond Head.

The rest of the flight was uneventful. The sky stayed clear all night and the next morning. The radio and all instruments worked perfectly. After 18 hours and 15 minutes, Earhart landed safely in Oakland, CA. A crowd of 10,000 people showed up to congratulate her. A cartoon appeared soon after in the Pittsburgh Post-Gazette, showing Earhart as a gangly tomboy jumping from Hawaii to California over the heads of seven famous male flyers. "Know any new stunts, fellers?" the cartoon Earhart asks.

After this flight she accepted an job as visiting aeronautics adviser at Purdue University in Indiana. Purdue was so impressed by her work that the university established the Amelia Earhart Research Foundation and used the funds to buy and maintain a twin-engine Lockheed Electra as a flying laboratory. This gave Earhart access to the sort of long-range craft she knew she needed for her next distance flight, an around-the-world trip. The Electra was intended for research flights to test effects of altitude on metabolism, the rate at which pilots became fatigued, and other scientific problems of flight. Earhart wanted to experiment with the reactions of men and women to long flights to see if there were any differences, as well as be the first to fly around the world over the longest route.

After studying maps and weather patterns and practicing instrument flying and emergency landing, Earhart decided she would need a navigator to help her plan the long Pacific flights. Putnam suggested Henry Bradford Washburn, Jr., who was the head of Harvard University's Institute of Geographical Exploration. After going over the maps and the route with Earhart, Washburn was astonished that she meant to hit tiny Howland Island in the middle of the Pacific by dead reckoning. He recommended a radio to assist with navigation. Putnam arranged to have a Coast Guard cutter off of Howland Island with a transmitter that could send a homing signal. Washburn, however, did not go on the flight.

Earhart took off from Oakland for Honolulu on March 17, 1937 with her long-time mechanic and advisor Paul Mantz, and navigators Harry Manning and Fred Noonan. The flight to Honolulu was uneventful, but on March 19, taking off for Howland, the Electra ground-looped on takeoff. The crew was unhurt, but the Electra was badly

Amelia Earhart stands in front of a Lockheed Electra 10E, before her last flight in 1937. She was reportedly lost at sea in mid-ocean.

damaged. Earhart had the plane shipped back to the Lockheed factory in Burbank. After more thought, Earhart decided to try again, but to fly the route from east to west.

On June 1, 1937, Earhart took off from Miami for

Puerto Rico, with Noonan as navigator. "I have a feeling there is just about one more good flight left in my system," Earhart said to a New York Herald Tribune reporter before takeoff, "and I hope this trip is it."

The radio system, however, had given them trouble. The aerials were shortened, which seemed to help, but Mantz, arriving after the flight had taken off, was horrified to find that the trailing aerial had not been installed, which might seriously impair their radio capabilities. However, the early part of the flight was carried off without incident. Earhart proceeded to Natal, and took off from Natal on June 7 over the Atlantic. As they flew, Earhart sent back messages to Putnam and the Herald Tribune: "Just crossing equator. 6,000 feet. Sun brilliant. Little lamb clouds below."

They crossed the Atlantic and flew across Africa and to India without any serious incident. After crossing southeast Asia, they made an overwater flight to Darwin, Australia, then across more water to Lae, New Guinea. At each planned stop there were 50-gallon drums of fuel labeled "Amelia Earhart" in red or white letters. Earhart's call letters, KHAQQ, were fast becoming as familiar as her name.

They had been flying 30 days since taking off from Miami, and were becoming fatigued, though the Electra was holding up well. The last leg, and the most hazardous, remained. Noonan was worried about the chronometers, which had to be set precisely, but he could not get exact time signals broadcast by the U.S. Navy and Bureau of Standards either from the Electra's radio nor the Lae airport. This concerned Earhart, too, because she knew that locating Howland was going to be difficult, and they needed all the navigation aids they could get. Earhart and Noonan took off from Lae on July 2 at 10:00 in the morning. The Coast Guard cutter *Itasca*, stationed near Howland Island, was alerted and began operation of the direction finder and the homing signal. Earhart was to transmit her call signal and flight information every 30 minutes.

At 5:20 New Guinea time, Earhart reported to Lae that she was past the Solomon Island and on course. Weather reports indicate that she was probably encountering strong head winds, but she reported no problems. She was almost a third of the way to Howland.

At 2:45 a.m., Howland time, Earhart radioed again, though there was heavy static. "KHAQQ... cloudy... weather cloudy." The *Itasca* proceeded with its transmission. At 3:45 a.m. she signaled again, and the signal was somewhat stronger. "*Itasca* from Earhart. *Itasca*. Broadcast 3105 kilocycles on hour and half-hour. Broadcast 3105 kilocycles on hour and half-hour. Overcast."

At 6:15, only 15 minutes from Howland, Earhart requested a radio bearing. She said she would whistle into the microphone so the *Itasca* could get a fix on her position, but her whistling was indistinguishable from the rest of the whines of the transmission. The crew asked for a longer transmission, but there was no reply.

The Electra's estimated time of arrival came and went, and still there was silence. Finally at 6:45 Earhart came in loud and clear: "Please take a bearing on us and report in half-hour. I will make noise in microphone. About 100 miles out." Again the signal was too short to get a bearing. The ship continued sending homing signals almost continuously, but there was no reply.

At 7:42 am, Earhart came in clearly. "KHAQQ calling *Itasca*. We must be on you but cannot see you. But gas is running low. Have been unable to reach you by radio. We are flying at 1,000 feet." The *Itasca* signaled back, but there was no response. At 7:58 Earhart came in again. "KHAQQ calling *Itasca*. We are circling but cannot see island, cannot hear you." She asked for a return transmission, and her voice sounded strained. The radiomen sent out a series of signals. Earhart broke in, responding at last. "We are receiving your signals. Please take bearing on us and answer at 3105 kilocycles." She sent a series of dots and dashes, but the *Itasca* called back saying they could not get a bearing. There was no reply.

The plane was two hours overdue. The *Itasca* sent up a plume of dark smoke that Earhart might spot. The radio operators continued calling. Earhart came on again at 8:45 a.m., sounding frantic. "We are on the line of position 157-337. We are running north and south." Then the radio went silent forever.

The *Itasca* began a search at 10:40 a.m., using Noonan's last calculated position which had probably been based on the sun's position. The aviators were most likely flying a search pattern in hopes of spotting the island. A larger sea search began soon after, involving 10 ships and numerous planes, which searched for days. But no trace of the Electra was ever found.

The story has inspired many fanciful explanations, some involving secret spy missions that Earhart was supposedly sent on. Stories sprang up after WWII, based on dubious eyewitness accounts, of the flyers being captured and executed by Japanese soldiers on Saipan or

Truk. But the most likely explanation is that the instruments failed in some way — perhaps the chronometers were inaccurate after all — and the flyers simply missed their target and were forced to ditch.

A memorial was held five months later at Floyd Bennet Field on Long Island, NY. Members of the Women's National Aeronautics Association gathered on a November morning. The speaker was Jacqueline Cochran, a well-known woman pilot who was a close friend of Earhart. Cochran said, "If her last flight was into eternity, one can mourn her loss but not regret her effort. Amelia did not lose, for her last flight was endless. Like in a relay race of progress, she had merely placed the torch in the hands of others to carry on to the next goal and from there on and forever."

Chapter 13
Wings Across Africa
— Beryl Markham

The Murani warriors called the child "Lakweit," the child who trotted after them, spear in hand, ready to join them in the hunt regardless of how dangerous the game might be. That the child was a girl was unusual enough, for no girl of their tribe hunted. What made her presence stranger still was that this girl was an English child.

Little "Lakweit" was born Beryl Clutterbuck in Ashwall, England in 1902. When she was only three, her father moved to Kenya where he intended to farm. Her brother became ill and returned with their mother to England, where they stayed. Beryl did not see them again until she was an adult.

The Charles Clutterbuck, Beryl's father, tried several different crops before he settled on horse breeding. He established a large ranch, hiring Africans as ranch hands. Beryl spent most of her time playing with Nandi children, enjoying the rough play of the boys most of all. From a very young age she slept in her own mud hut in the ranch compound, with only her dog, Buller, for protection. Once a leopard broke into the compound and tried to drag Buller away. Beryl ran for help, and her father tracked the animals down. They found Buller lying wounded with a hole in his jaw and another in his head, but still alive. The dog recovered later. The leopard, however, had gotten the worst of the fight. Men from the ranch found the big cat soon after with one ear missing and its throat badly torn.

Young Beryl had many adventures on the African highlands of which few English girls could boast. She was once attacked by a lion which a nearby rancher kept as a pet, narrowly escaping with her life when the men of the ranch ran to help her. She hunted wild boars with the Murani, the warriors of the Nandi people. Once while riding out on her mare, a zebra foal followed her home. She tried to raise the foal herself, feeding it from a bottle, but the young and headstrong zebra decided all bottles on the ranch were his personal property. When he started chasing Beryl's father every time he had a bottle of beer in his hand, the elder Clutterbuck said the foal had to go.

Her only schooling consisted of a brief period at an English school in Nairobi, beginning in 1913. Beryl missed the complete freedom she'd enjoyed on the ranch and refused to obey school rules. She had been raised on the Njoro highlands and believed without question that only the strongest survived. How could pencils and paper protect her from predators? What could books teach her that the Murani could not about tracking, killing, and skinning game? She was asked to leave, and never attended school again. Her father tried several governesses, but Beryl ignored them all.

Life on the ranch began to change in 1915 when the first World War erupted in Europe. Many men from the area, European and African alike, went off to the front in German East Africa. Some never returned. A drought a few years later nearly ruined the Clutterbuck enterprise when Beryl's father honored contracts to deliver flour from his mill at a fixed price, and was forced to buy the grain at a much higher price than he could sell it for. He decided to leave Africa and resettle in Peru. He advised Beryl to stay in Africa, and to hire as a horse trainer in a nearby community. Though only in her teens, Beryl was on her own.

She took a job as a horse trainer in Molo, despite the fact that horse training was considered to be a man's job, and a tough job at that. But her early training in survival and competition weren't for nothing. She found a job and held her own among the men she competed with.

She also found a husband. In 1919, though still barely eighteen, she married Jock Purves, an Englishman. The marriage did not last, however. The two divorced in 1924. Beryl continued working as a horse trainer in Molo. There she met pilot Tom Black, with whom she would form a lifelong friendship.

Black was driving across Kenya when his car broke down and he was forced into Molo for repairs. He told Beryl stories about flying, and though she had never seen an airplane in her life, she was captivated. But horses were her life at the time, and she continued as a trainer at Molo and later at Nakuru.

In 1927, Beryl tried marriage again, this time to wealthy Mansfield Markham, a horse breeder in Kenya. The marriage was brief. Undoubtedly she enjoyed the period of luxury, including a honeymoon in Paris. However, the birth of her son, Gervas, in 1929 was more than she could bear. She had grown up motherless and felt no maternal instincts. Further, the boy was born with a deformity that required several operations to repair. In the culture of the Africans she'd grown up with, a child born deformed was left out in the open. Only if it survived the pounding hooves of the tribe's cattle as they were driven to pasture would the tribe decide that the child was meant to live. Trying to help the child with operations made no sense to her. Beryl felt that the sickly boy was too weak to survive in the African wilds. She returned to Africa alone later in 1929, leaving her son with her mother-in-law to be raised.

She met up with Tom Black again in Nairobi. Black had just returned from a rescue mission to an ill-fated safari. Three hunters from Europe had shot a lion which had been raised from a cub to be nothing more than a target for white hunters. They'd failed to kill it and decided instead to photograph its death agonies. The lion turned on them, killing one of the men and maiming a second. The dead hunter had to be cremated on the spot. Black had flown the survivors back to Nairobi, along with the ashes of the dead hunter, deposited in a tin box. Beryl sat talking with Black far into the night, and was soon convinced that flying would be her next career.

It wasn't only Black's talk that convinced her. Beryl had been in love with a pilot named Denys Finch Hatton, who was also an avid hunter. Not long before Beryl's conversation with Black, Hatton had been killed in a plane crash. Beryl believed, as the Africans who raised her had, that all things had to be paid for. Perhaps Hatch's death had been the price she must pay for his love, and in return, she would take up his flying career.

Black taught Beryl in a D.H. Gipsy Moth. Eighteen months later, with over a thousand flying hours behind her, she earned her "B," or professional, license on July 13, 1931.

Beryl took to free-lance flying, taking passengers, mail supplies, or whatever she could be hired to fly. As soon as she had the money, she bought a Leopard Moth which seated two passengers instead of one, which increased the money she could earn. She charged a shilling per mile per passenger. The Leopard also had a closed cabin, which was more appealing to her passengers.

By 1935, Black had left Kenya, leaving Beryl as the only professional pilot in the country. She was also the only female pilot in all of Africa.

Beryl formed a friendship with Baron von Blixen, a hunter and safari organizer who went by the name of "Blix." Beryl would scout out elephants and other game in the area from the air, and report back to Blix. Aerial scouting was dangerous business because the country was so rough. Sansiveria bushes had sharp leaves that could pierce the canvas sides of airplanes. In addition, the elephants were clever. The cows would often mass around the bulls, hiding their tusks so that the aerial scouts could not tell for sure if there were bull in the herd. Sometimes Beryl would spot the hindquarters of an elephant sticking out of the brush and circle until the elephant moved and she saw it was a cow. Beryl swore the cow posed as a distraction while the herd got away.

Beryl heard that Tom Black was competing in a long-distance air race from London to Australia. She got to thinking about long-distance flying herself, and thought she might like to see England again. Blix agreed to fly with her.

The flight was arduous, as Italy had control of much of Northern Africa at the time, and the Italian government had set up numerous checkpoints from Cairo all across the northern part of the continent. Beryl and Blix were required to stop at every one of them. At last they were able to cross the Mediterranean into France, then fly north to England.

In London, Beryl dined with a friend, John Carberry, an Irishman who also had a home in Kenya. During dinner, the conversation turned to record-breaking flights. June Carberry suggested that her husband ought to finance a long distance flight, and Beryl ought to fly it. The year was 1936, and at that point Amelia Earhart was the only woman who had flown across the Atlantic. Though many pilots had crossed that ocean from west to east, no one had successfully flown east to west. Carberry said that if Beryl wanted to break a record, that was the flight to make.

Beryl ordered a Vega Gull to be built for her. The plane was a standard sport model, with a range of about 660 miles, but was modified to carry extra fuel. The *Messenger*, as it was called, was turquoise with silver wings. Beryl herself supervised its construction at Gravesend, England. While she waited for a suitable time to take off, she trained like an athlete to prepare herself for the grueling flight.

On September 4, 1936, despite a gloomy weather forecast, Beryl took off from Abingdon on the west coast of England just before nightfall. The Carberrys had already sailed to New York to be there when she arrived. Fog, rain, and storms greeted her in the first hours of her flight. Heavy headwinds reduced her speed to ninety miles an hour. At that rate, the flight would take more than thirty hours, and the *Messenger* was already eating up fuel faster than she had anticipated. She had no radio, so no way of contacting either mainland. What was worse, a gas line developed a slow leak and gas fumes filled the cabin, making it hard to concentrate.

Four hours into the flight, the engine quit when the first fuel tank went dry. Five tanks remained. Beryl knew she was using up fuel too quickly. She switched to a fresh tank, which bore the written assurance that it had four hours worth of gasoline in it. Only an hour and thirty-five minutes later the engine died again. Beryl fumbled in the dark for the petcock to another tank, while putting the plane into a dive in an attempt to start up the engine again. Finally, at a dangerously low altitude, the engine started up again and Beryl could nose up and gain altitude once more.

At daybreak she spotted the cliffs of Newfoundland. She had been flying blind for nineteen hours. Ice formed on the glass of the windscreen, cutting off her forward vision. Fog obscured the coastline and Beryl navigated by map and compass.

The engine died once more over the coastline. Later she would find that there was ice in the fuel line from the last tank, but at the time all she knew was that she was out of fuel. Beryl kept turning the petcocks until her hands bled in an effort to get fuel to the engine. It finally started up again, but continued dying each time she descended to get her bearings.

At last she found land again. She figured she was about twelve minutes from the Sydney Airport, her immediate destination. The engine cut once again and she glided, thinking she could gain altitude again and start it up. This time, however, she could not restart the engine. She glided to the flattest spot she could find. The earth was soft and the plane's wheels sank, upending the Vega. Beryl was thrown against the windscreen and cut her forehead. She stumbled out of the plane and looked at her watch. Twenty-one hours and twenty minutes had passed since she had taken off from England. A local fisherman spotted her after she'd been wandering the bog for an hour. He directed her out and took her to his home, where she was able to telephone the Sydney airport.

A few days later she flew into Floyd Bennett Field in New York, wishing she were doing so in her *Messenger*. The cheering crowds didn't seem to care what she was flying. She had made the crossing, and that was enough.

Beryl decided to stay in the United States for a while. In 1942 she published an autobiography, *West With the Night*. While the book describes her bush pilot days in Africa, and her Atlantic crossing in detail, there is much that she left out — including her marriages and the birth of her son. Later, her authorship was called into question. While she undoubtedly kept complete notes and wrote the first chapters, it is likely that her third husband, Raoul Schumacher, assisted with the completion of the book. Schumacher was a writer himself, and edited her work on *West With the Night*. Later, after their divorce, Schumacher claimed he wrote the entire book himself. How much each of the two contributed to the final book may never be known.

Beryl moved to California, where she ran an avocado plantation for several years. In 1952 she returned to Kenya, and from the late 1950's until 1972 she was one of the most successful horse ranchers in the country. However, she had as little regard for money as the Africans she had been raised among. Only actual livestock had value for her. She gave so little attention to finances that by 1980 she had lost everything and was living in poverty. Then in 1983 a letter by the famous writer Ernest Hemingway was discovered, and in it was a reference to Beryl's autobiography. The book was found and republished, renewing Beryl's fame and bringing in much-needed income. Though she was in her eighties, she still rose at dawn on the African highlands to train her horses, just as she had since she was a child. She died in Kenya in 1986 at the age of 83.

Chapter 14
Mid-Air Oil Change
— Charles Kingsford-Smith and P.G. Taylor

First to fly across the southern Pacific. First to fly nonstop across Australia. First to fly from Australia to New Zealand. In his career as a pilot, Charles Kingsford-Smith had already racked up an impressive list of courageous firsts in his tri-motor Fokker, the *Southern Cross*. But none of these achievements could top the daring adventure that took place during the flight that Kingsford-Smith *didn't* complete.

Kingsford-Smith made his trans-Pacific flight in the *Southern Cross* in 1928, flying from island to island south of the equator. He continued flying the same plane on his subsequent long-distance flights. By 1935, the tri-motor Fokker was showing her age, yet Kingsford-Smith thought she still had another good flight left in her. Flying was still considered a dangerous sport in 1935, and Kingsford-Smith wanted to prove to Australians that air travel could connect them to the rest of the world. That was why he chose his famous plane for the first air mail run from Australia to New Zealand.

The response to his announcement of the flight was enormous. Citizens from all over Australia composed a total of 29,000 letters to be carried on the flight. Kingsford-Smith chose P.G. Taylor, an experienced combat flyer and airline pilot who knew the South Pacific better than any other flyer, as his co-pilot. In addition to being an excellent pilot, Taylor was also a skilled navigator. Kingsford-Smith also hired John Stannage as a radio operator. The three-man crew set out in the evening of May 14th from Australia's east coast with their mail load, heading to New Zealand, 1,500 miles away across empty ocean.

Taylor was at the controls at dawn, and was the first to notice trouble. Just ahead of the cockpit, on the manifold of the center engine, Taylor noticed a white-hot, glowing spot. The instruments registered normal, however, so Taylor kept on flying. When Kingsford-Smith came forward from passing messages back to Stannage, Taylor pointed out the glowing spot. As they watched, the manifold exploded into flames. The plane shook violently, as though it would tear to pieces, as the right engine suddenly vibrated wildly.

Kingsford-Smith quickly shut down the right engine, and the men saw the problem immediately. One of the propeller blades was broken. Part of the manifold must have hit the propeller in the explosion. With one blade sheared off, the propeller was out of balance. But without the power of the right engine, the plane began a slow descent.

The *Southern Cross* was nearly halfway across the Tasman Sea at that point, with no help in sight. Bitterly, Kingsford-Smith decided that they would have to give up the trip and return to Australia, as the Australian coast was closer than New Zealand. Taylor calculated the new course, and Kingsford-Smith turned the craft around. But the plane was still sinking. The crew needed to lighten the load.

Taylor went to the back of the plane, and with the help

of Stannage, tossed out everything that wasn't immediately needed — luggage, freight, even tools. It still wasn't enough. Kingsford-Smith calculated the amount of fuel they would need to reach Australia, and dumped the excess. At last the plane rose.

The pilots settled in for the long flight back. Stannage radioed the Sydney airfield, and learned that rescue ships were heading toward them, but were still hours away. Taylor and Kingsford-Smith took turns at the controls, letting each other rest and stay fresh.

At least, Taylor thought, the worst was over, and he cut back on the throttle to relieve the strain on the engine. But his thought was premature. The needle on the oil pressure gauge to the left engine suddenly dropped. The engine was leaking oil, and and the rate the pressure was falling, the engine would cut out in less than fifteen minutes. The crewmen prepared to ditch in the ocean, and Stannage radioed their position to their rescuers.

As Kingsford-Smith pulled off his heavy flying boots in preparation, a thought suddenly occurred to Taylor. The crippled right engine was still full of oil! If he could somehow get the oil from the right engine to the left, he could prolong the flight, possibly enough to get the plane back to the Australian coast. At least they could get closer to the rescue crews that were on their way.

Before Kingsford-Smith could stop him, Taylor was halfway out the side window, yelling that he was going to get some oil. The slipstream was strong, but Taylor held on tightly to the struts that supported the fixed landing gear, and inched his way across to the engine. At one point there were no handholds, and Taylor had to brace his shoulder against the bottom of the wing and his feet on

Sir Charles Kingsford-Smith (right) and his co-pilot, Capt. P.G. Taylor, after landing at Oakland, California on their flight from Australia to California in 1934.

the strut, sidestepping cautiously until he reached the engine.

Once there, he pulled off the engine cowling, which blew off in the slipstream. He tried to unscrew the drain plug, but it was on too tight, and regretfully he remembered dropping the toolbox into the sea when they lightened the plane's load. Stannage came to the rescue, however, when he found a spare wrench that had been overlooked in the cockpit. By reaching out as far as he could, Stannage was able to pass the wrench to Taylor so that the co-pilot didn't have to make the trip back.

Once the oil plug was loose, the next problem was to find something to put the oil in. Again, Stannage solved the problem. He rummaged around until he found an empty thermos flask that had held coffee, and passed it out to the co-pilot. Taylor filled it as best he could. Oil sprayed out, blown by the slipstream, and made the struts treacherously slick. Taylor held on, and passed the flask back to Stannage. The flask only held a few cups of oil, not nearly enough to save the faltering engine. Once more, the resourceful Stannage solved the problem. He grabbed a leather suitcase full of maps and dumped out the contents, then poured the flask of oil into it. He passed the flask back to Taylor.

When the suitcase was full of oil, Taylor edged back along the slippery strut and back into the cockpit, where he collapsed from exhaustion. He couldn't afford to rest now, though. The oil pressure in the left engine was perilously low and the engine might seize up at any moment. Taylor got to his feet and put one foot out the left window. With the left engine running, however, the slipstream was too strong, and Taylor was knocked back into the cockpit.

Kingsford-Smith decided to take a chance on cutting the left engine, though the plane would be seriously underpowered and would sink fast. He took the *Southern Cross* up to 700 feet, then shut the engine off. As the plane dropped, Taylor slipped out the left window and hustled across the struts to the engine. As fast as Stannage could pass the oil, Taylor poured it into the engine. Before he could finish, the plane was almost to the sea. Kingsford-Smith signaled Taylor to hold on and turned the engine on. He took the plane up again, and shut the engine off so that Taylor could finish the job. Kingsford-Smith had to turn the engine on once more before they were done, but when he shut it down again, Taylor inched back across the struts and fell back into the cockpit, drenched with oil and exhausted.

His risky plan had succeeded. The engine pressure was back up where it belonged and the left engine was working normally. Stannage radioed a message to Sydney saying that the *Southern Cross* was still in the air.

However, thirty minutes later the oil pressure in the left engine dropped again. Taylor repeated his performance, inching out on the oil-slick struts to pass precious oil from the right engine to the left. The crew still needed to lighten the load in order to make it back safely. The only thing left to dump was the mail. It was the hardest blow of the trip, as the men had hoped to win approval of a regular air mail run between Australia and New Zealand, but it had to be done.

But their problems weren't over yet. Though Taylor had refilled the engine with oil, the leak had not been fixed, and the oil pressure dropped again. Before the flight was done, Taylor had to make five exhausting trips to transfer oil from the right engine to the left.

It wasn't until about three in the afternoon that they spotted the eastern coast of Australia. Just thirty miles off the coast, Taylor made his last oil transfer. Kingsford-Smith took the crippled plane into the Sydney airport soon after, where they were greeted by cheering crowds. Australian citizens had been following the hair-raising adventure of the *Southern Cross* on the radio, and were relieved and elated that the crew had arrived safely.

A smiling Douglas Corrigan steps out of his plane just after one of the strangest flights in history.

Chapter 15
"Wrong Way" Gets His Wish
— Douglas Corrigan

The day that Douglas Corrigan shook hands with Charles Lindbergh, a dream was born.

Corrigan was just another worker at the Ryan Aircraft company at the time, and the craft that the crew had recently finished was the *Spirit of St. Louis*, the plane that Lindbergh later flew solo from New York to Paris. Corrigan helped assemble the wings, install the instruments, and worked on the final assembly process.

But Corrigan didn't just build planes. He flew them. Every spare moment and spare dollar he had went into flying. And flying across the Atlantic to fame appealed to him more than anything else.

Corrigan was born in 1907 in Galveston, Texas. His father was a civil engineer and an inventor, though none of his inventions turned out to be practical. For extra money, he bought empty lots near their home, built houses on them, and sold them at a profit. With the money he earned from real estate he was able to quit his job and open up a candy shop. He continued buying lots and building houses.

When Corrigan was about nine, Texas was hit with a housing slump. His father lost money on the houses and borrowed against the candy shop to make ends meet. One night he announced he was going on a business trip. He never returned, and later filed for divorce. The house, store, and furniture were repossessed, leaving Mrs. Corrigan with three children and nothing else. She borrowed money from her family and opened a boarding house, which brought in just enough to keep the family alive. Douglas worked after school selling newspapers to help the family.

After the first World War, Texas went through another economic slump. Mrs. Corrigan decided to move her family to California where prospects were better. She found a boarding house to manage which gave her a larger income than before so that her sons didn't have to go back to selling newspapers.

The summer after Corrigan finished eighth grade his mother fell sick. Corrigan took a job in an apricot cannery and earned enough money to see the family through the summer, but the cannery went out of business shortly after. Mrs. Corrigan found out she had cancer and needed an operation. She decided to move in with her family in Pittsburgh. On the advice of her relatives, she sent the boys to live with their father who had since remarried and lived in New York. They stayed ten months, and Corrigan completed the ninth grade, though his heart wasn't in his studies.

Mrs. Corrigan asked for her boys back and moved the family back to California in 1921. Corrigan took a job in a soda water plant while his brother Harry sold newspapers and his sister Evelyn helped at home. Corrigan progressed in the company until he was making $25 a week, which felt like riches.

But no amount of money could cure Mrs. Corrigan's cancer. When she died, Evelyn went to live with an aunt and uncle. Corrigan thought he could support himself and his brother. He took jobs in construction, taking whatever positions he could find.

One evening as he came home from a job, he saw airplanes for the first time in his life as they took off from a newly-constructed field. He was fascinated. That Sunday, instead of staying home to read as he usually did, he went out to the airfield. By the following Sunday he had scraped up enough money to pay for a short ride.

He arrived at the airfield with five dollars in his pocket and asked how much lessons cost. The field manager told him it was twenty dollars an hour, with fifteen minutes being the shortest lesson. Corrigan paid for a fifteen minute lesson on the spot.

Corrigan returned every Sunday for his short lesson. After the lesson was over, he would hang out with the mechanic, learning everything he could about how the airplanes worked. After five months of lessons, he soloed for the first time on March 25, 1926.

Corrigan got serious flight training when he joined the California National Guard. There he took classes in airplane repair and engine overhauls. During summer training, Corrigan took his first cross-country flights and took part in formation flying. Corrigan saw friends go off to become flying cadets in the U.S. Army, but since he had not completed high school, he could not attend.

As the housing industry declined in California, Corrigan looked for other work. He took off for San Diego, leaving his brother behind to finish high school, and looked for flying jobs where he could find them. Eventually he was hired as a mechanic for the Ryan company.

One day another mechanic called Corrigan out to help

get one of the monoplanes started. The mechanic pointed to the pilot and said, "This is a fellow from St. Louis that wants to fly from New York to Paris."

Corrigan took a look. "Gosh, he looks like a farmer. Do you suppose he can fly?"

"We'll find out pretty soon," the mechanic replied. "He's going to take this ship up."

They watched the pilot come down the field 200 feet above the ground, head upwind, and do nine consecutive loops with a wingover at the end. He brought the plane down, and Corrigan and the mechanic agreed he could probably fly well enough, since it was the best low-altitude stunting they had seen. They asked who he was and found out his name was Charles Lindbergh, and that he liked the plane well enough that he wanted one built for him.

Lindbergh had ordered a modification of the Ryan Brougham, and the order was a rush job since other pilots wanted to make the flight and Lindbergh wanted to beat them.

Corrigan and another worker were transferred to the factory to help out. For two months Corrigan worked on wing ribs, wing assembly, installation of gas tanks and lines, covering the wings with fabric, doping the fabric cover, and assembly of parts. He also installed the instrument board with a tachometer, altimeter, air-speed indicator, engine oil-pressure gauge, bank-and-turn indicator, and oil-temperature gauge. An earth-indicator compass was located on the rear of the fuselage, and an ordinary magnetic compass was installed first on the floor of the plane, then overhead. The plane's final assembly took place outside in the field. While several other workers held the wings up, Corrigan pulled the fuselage underneath and bolted the wings in place. The plane was completed on April 28, 1927 and Lindbergh tested it the same day. When the news reached San Diego that Lindbergh had reached Paris, the whole city celebrated. The factory workers jumped into cars and went driving through the streets of San Diego, waving.

Following Lindbergh's flight, the factory got more orders than it could handle. The workforce went from 20 to 120, and the factory was turning out five-seat cabin planes at a rate of three a week. Corrigan trained to be a welder. He worked six days a week, and didn't always get to fly on Sundays since he was saving to buy his own plane.

Corrigan met Lindbergh again in June of 1928, the second time since Lindbergh completed his flight. The first time had been at the end of a nationwide tour. This time, he came to inspect a new plane that the company was building for him. Corrigan shook hands with him and spoke a few words. In those moments, the young factory worker felt inspired to finally do what had been a crazy dream ever since Lindbergh took his flight — to fly the Atlantic himself. Yet he kept on at the factory, not yet ready to throw down his welding torch and chase after a dream.

Corrigan continued working as a mechanic while he studied for a transport license so that he could fly passenger planes. Then, in 1929, the Great Depression hit. Jobs were scarce everywhere. Corrigan took work at any airfield that would hire him, either as a mechanic or a pilot, working hard to keep his brother in college and his sister in school, as well as saving for his own dream.

Corrigan wanted an airplane of his own.

When he had enough money saved up, Corrigan and fellow pilot Steve Reich bought two planes and a hangar at Fitzmaurice Field on Long Island and went into business for themselves in 1931. Though they had only a few students and passenger business was slow, they owned the hangar outright so they had no rent to pay. Corrigan's brother Harry came to Long Island when he finished school and work for them for a while, selling tickets to passengers.

Eventually Corrigan got tired of New York. He bought a Curtiss Robin and, with his brother, flew it to Los Angeles, selling airplane rides along the way to pay for the journey. All through 1934 he worked in the Northrop and Douglas airplane factories whenever there was work. He rented a hangar for his Curtiss Robin, and slept in the hangar to save on rent. In January of 1935, out of work for the third time in eight months, he went back to the Ryan company.

By October, Corrigan found all the promises of good pay and moving up weren't coming true. He started fixing up the Robin, thinking now might be a good time to try the Atlantic flight he'd dreamed of since meeting Lindbergh. He got permission from the chief inspector in Los Angeles to upgrade the engine, but not for the bigger gas tanks that he needed.

The next few years were full of delays and broken promises as Corrigan tried his hardest to get permission to fly the Atlantic and to get the equipment he needed to have the Robin ready for the trip. He was told he would need an instrument rating and would have to get a radio license also, even though his plane had no radio. He sent his application to fly direct from New York to London, but about that time Amelia Earhart was lost in the Pacific on an attempted around-the-world flight. Corrigan was told that there would be no more permissions granted for oceanic flights. His license for his plane was also refused. Despite the delays, Corrigan took his plane on several long-distance overland flights, not only to practice but to prove that the aging Robin was up to the challenge. About this time he painted his plane yellow and named it *Sunshine*, since it had always been a ray of sunshine in his life.

Corrigan asked the chief inspector for permission to make a non-stop flight from New York to Los Angeles and a non-stop flight to return. The inspector finally agreed to permit the flight east, and, if Corrigan made it, would approve the return flight. The plane passed inspection and was licensed. On July 7, 1938, Corrigan took off with 100 gallons of fuel and told the crew at the airport that he was flying to Texas for a few days. He flew to Long Beach and asked for 145 gallons more and said he was going on a test-hop to El Paso. That way no one knew he had enough fuel for the cross-country flight, and if he didn't make it, no one would know the flight was a failure.

Over the Cumberland Mountains he was flying blind through rainstorms. One of the gas tanks developed a slow leak. Corrigan had to open a window for fresh air to keep from falling asleep and to disperse the fumes. At sundown on July 9th, Corrigan landed at Roosevelt Field in New York with only four gallons of fuel left, and parked the plane in Steve Reich's hangar. A reporter asked where he had just come from and Corrigan said,

"Long Beach." The report wasn't impressed until he noticed the big tanks and began to put things together, realizing Corrigan had meant California and not Long Beach, New York

During the next few days, Corrigan stayed at the field and cleaned up the plane, replacing engine parts that were worn. On the next Saturday, Corrigan saw that the weather across the country looked good, with easterly winds across Texas that would help him along. He stowed his belongings, two boxes of fig cookies, two chocolate bars, and a quart of water into the *Sunshine*. He asked Steve Reich to tell his brother Harry that he would be back to see him in a week or two. He intended to come back east for work. American Airlines also wanted him to make an eastern flight, stopping at all their stations on the southern route if he completed the flight from New York to Los Angeles non-stop.

Corrigan flew to Floyd Bennet field on Saturday evening and put the plane in a hangar for last-minute maintenance. He told the hangar boy to gas up the plane because he meant to take off shortly after midnight. He got word that he could not get permission to take off until morning. At 4 a.m., permission finally came through. When the plane was out of the hangar and the motor started, Corrigan asked the manager, "Which way shall I take off?"

"Any direction you want," came the fateful reply, "except don't head towards the buildings on the west side of the field."

"I'll take off east," Corrigan said. He rolled down the runway for about 3000 feet and took off toward the Atlantic. Those who were watching from the ground figured he would turn westward once he was in the air.

But the *Sunshine* did not turn. It disappeared into a fog bank, continuing on an easterly course out over the Atlantic.

For the rest of his life, Corrigan swore that he simply misread the new-style compass and thought he was heading west. He later reported seeing trees below him and, thinking he was over Baltimore, kept flying. The clouds kept getting higher, and Corrigan flew to 4000 feet to get above them.

Ten hours into the flight his feet were cold. He saw that the leak in the main gas tank was worse and fuel was dribbling down over his shoes. Fifteen hours out of New York he was at 6000 feet, above clouds, and it became dark. With no horizon to watch, Corrigan had to pay attention to the turn indicator and air speed to keep the plane level.

Later than night he saw the leak was even worse. There was a puddle of gas an inch deep in the bottom of the plane. Worried that a leak on the left side would dribble gas on the hot exhaust pipe on that side, he punched a hole in the bottom of the plane on the right side with a screwdriver.

When morning came, Corrigan was at 8000 feet and still above the clouds. Ahead, the clouds towered up to 15,000 feet. Corrigan did not want to fly that high, so he dropped into the clouds and flew by instruments. It was getting colder, and Corrigan dropped lower to try to prevent ice from building up on the plane. He kept dropping cautiously. At 3,500 feet he came down beneath the clouds and saw nothing but water underneath.

He spotted a small fishing boat and flew close, but no

one came up on deck. He kept going straight ahead, figuring a small boat like that would not be far from a shoreline. He opened up his food finally and had plowed his way through the fig bars when he saw green hills ahead. He saw no towns, so flew inland and in 45 minutes came to another shore. To his right he saw a city and headed for it, but did not see an airport. In another half-hour he spotted a fighter plane. It drew up alongside him, then pulled in front and disappeared. A few minutes later he saw a large city under him and an airport to the right. The name "Baldonnel" was marked in the center of the field. Corrigan knew this was in Dublin. He circled twice to check wind direction, then put down.

After asking if he had landed in the right field, he said to the Army officer who greeted him, "My name's Corrigan. I left New York yesterday morning headed for California, but I got mixed up in the clouds and must have flown the wrong way."

The officer said, "Yes, we know."

Corrigan was surprised and asked how he found out.

"Oh, there was a small piece in the paper saying you might be flying over this way, and just a few minutes ago we got a phone call from Belfast saying a plane with American markings had flown over and was headed down the coast."

The army officer arranged for Corrigan to be driven to the American Legation near Dublin. There, the American Minister interviewed him. Corrigan explained that he had taken off from New York, but must have misread the compass, and in the fog and haze he hadn't noticed that he'd flown over the ocean.

"It was hazy when you took off, was it?" the minister

said. "Well, your story seems a little hazy, too. Now come on and tell me the real story."

Corrigan insisted that *was* the real story, and that if the technical experts got to questioning him, he would show them the special compass and how easy it was to misread it.

"So you're sticking to that story, are you, hey?" the American minister asked.

"That's my story," Corrigan replied, "but I sure am ashamed of that navigation."

After a grand tour of Ireland and England, Corrigan returned home. On the way he received a cablegram telling him that his pilot's license was suspended until August 4th — the very day he was due to return to New York.

New Yorkers greeted him with a ticker-tape parade, and gave him the nickname of "Wrong-Way Corrigan." Corrigan toured the United States in the *Sunshine*, giving speeches wherever he stopped. When the tour was over, Corrigan turned his plane over to the California World's Fair officials, took an airliner to Los Angeles where he agreed to appear in a movie, then flew to New York where he wrote magazine articles.

Later in life, Corrigan bought an orange grove in California, which he farmed until he retired. He never changed his story about his flight, and all his life insisted that he had not purposely flown the Atlantic, but had only misread the compass. He wrote the story of his flight in 1938, titling his autobiographical work, *That's My Story* — and he's sticking to it!

Where to Learn More

Stories of these famous pilots and more can be found in your library and on the internet. Enter your favorite flyer's name into a search engine, or start with these aviation web sites:

Aero Web
http://www.aero-web.org/

All Star Network
http://www.allstar.fiu.edu/

American Aviation Hall of Fame
http://www.nationalaviation.org

Aviation History
http://www.aviation-history.com/

Bleriot.com
http://bleriot.com

Charles Lindbergh web site
http://www.charleslindbergh.com

Glenn Curtiss Museum
http://www.linkny.com/CurtissMuseum/

The Harriet Quimby Research Conference
http://www.harrietquimby.org/

Hubert Latham web site
http://www.latham77.fsnet.co.uk/

Lincoln Beachey web site
http://lincolnbeachey.com/

The National Air and Space Museum
http://www.nasm.edu

Wright Brothers Aeroplane Company and Museum of Pioneer Aviation
http://www.first-to-fly.com

Index

Abbot, Robert 80, 82
Baldwin, Thomas Scott 22-25, 30, 33-34
Barnes, Florence "Pancho" 114-15
Bell, Alexander Graham 25-27
Betsch, John Thomas 85-86
Black, Tom 127-29
Byrd, Admiral Richard E. 103-05, 110
Carberry, John 130
Clutterbuck, Charles 125-26
Damoth, Bill 23
Farman, Henri 34
Fowler, Robert 50, 55-56
Gordon, Lou 111-12
Guest, Mrs. Frederick 110
Hamel, Gustav 66
Hearst, William Randolph 50, 54, 57
Hill, Hezakiah Keith 85-86
Hill, Viola 85-86
Knaubenshue, Roy 23, 34, 59
Langley, Samuel P. 7-8, 10, 25, 41
Lilienthal, Otto 8, 10-12, 19, 47
Markham, Mansfield 127
Moisant, John 63
Moisant, Matilde 63-65
Nichols, Ruth 110, 114-115
Noonan, Fred 119, 121-23
Northcliffe, Lord 21, 45-47
Oldfield, Barney 41
Orteig, Raymond 102-04, 108
Putnam, George 115, 117, 119, 121
Read, Lt. Cmmdr. Albert 32, 99
Selfridge, Thomas 14-15
Stultz, Wilmer 111-13
Taylor, Charles 11, 53-54
Trout, Bobbi 114-15

von Blixen, Baron 129
Ward, Jimmy 50, 55-56
Willard, William 68
Wils, William 85-86

Alpena County Library
211 N. First Ave.
Alpena, MI 49707